"Jim PathFinder Ewing has a : to the roots of traditions, the draw their healing strength. In *to Out-of-Body Healing*, PathFin Reiki and Shamanism and den. ... authoritatively the deep relationship that they share and the healing harmonic that can be established through the practice of both. Throughout the book he shares his personal experiences of healing from the heart of these traditions and brings a new sense of unlimited possibility to Mother Earth and all of her children. Accessible and comprehensive, *Reiki Shamanism* is an inspiring book for practitioners and a delightful introduction to those beginning a healing quest."

—*Dana Robinson, Certified Shamanic Counselor, Faculty Member, Foundation for Shamanic Studies*

"Jim fully explains the hidden teachings of chakra anatomy and Reiki origins. Whether you are a beginner in 'hands on healing' or a seasoned healer, this book integrates ancient knowledge, scientific research, healing methods and exercises for each of us to learn from. I so enjoyed his comparative analysis of Reiki, Buddhism and Native American shamanism. I agree with Jim as he says, 'Reiki itself is a form of shamanism; there really is no separation between them.' From his heart he shares what our ancestors have lived since the beginning of time; to be one with our Mother Earth and to heal each other."

—*Melynda Ruckels, RN, Ph.D., Reiki Master/Teacher, faculty member, the Ritberger Institute, member, Board of Directors of Healing Hands Healing Hearts, Sacramento, CA*

by the same author

ISBN
978-1-84409-082-2

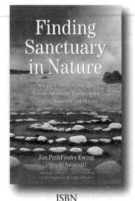

ISBN
978-1-84409-095-2

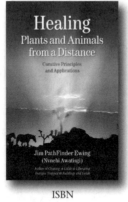

ISBN
978-1-84409-111-9

available from your local bookstore
or directly from www.findhornpress.com

Reiki Shamanism

A Guide to Out-of-Body Healing

Jim PathFinder Ewing
(Nvnehi Awatisgi)

FINDHORN PRESS

First published by Findhorn Press 2008

ISBN 978-1-84409-133-1

British Library Cataloguing-in-Publication Data.
A catalogue record for this book is available from the British Library.

Edited by Annette Waya Ewing and Michael Hawkins
Proof-read by Michael Hawkins
Cover design by Damian Keenan
Illustrations by Annette Waya Ewing
Layout by Pam Bochel
Printed in the USA

2 3 4 5 6 7 8 9 10 11 12 13 12 11 10 09

Published by
Findhorn Press
305A The Park,
Findhorn, Forres
Scotland IV36 3TE

t +44(0)1309 690582
f +44(0)131 777 2711
e info@findhornpress.com
www.findhornpress.com

To the Good Medicine in each and every being,
People, places and things,
Creator's Light
That connects us to Earth and Sky,
As Children walking between the worlds

As Children of Earth and Sky,
we see what Creator provides,
as Creator would have us see,
being as Earthly Mother would have us be,
one with all, in balance, peace and harmony.
That is the right way of the world, in healing,
health and wholeness.

Contents

Preface

Becoming a Reiki Shaman

"The universe is infinite. That boggles the mind, doesn't it? Beyond imagining. But, consider: Wherever you stand in infinity, you are in the center of it. The Creator made each and every one of us this way. We must only realize our uniqueness — and what we share: infinite being. At its center, each one of us."

— Ascension Tests[1]

The fist time I practiced Reiki while in the shamanic journey, it began so subtly, that I really wasn't aware it was happening until I saw the healing Reiki energy as a flowing purple radiance from my outstretched hands. This is incredible, I said to myself, as I saw the powerful energy reaching out to the person before me.

Why hasn't anyone written about this? Told anyone? Taught this? I wondered. Practicing both together is surprisingly simple, in many ways easier to attain than proficiency in either of the modalities alone.

I had been studying shamanism for more than 30 years, but Reiki was new to me, discovered late in life. The more I studied Reiki, the more I experienced a truth that few seemed willing to admit: Reiki is a form of shamanism. Combining the essential techniques of Reiki — using the symbols to channel healing energy — with the shamanic journey can be a perfect unfolding of both. Reiki may have had its roots grounded firmly in shamanism, but allowing Reiki "back" into shamanism is a natural progression toward a greater fulfillment of both healing modalities, as one. It is as natural to teach Reiki shamanism as to teach the separate modalities of Reiki and shamanism; combined, Reiki shamanism is greater in effect than either, yet as simple to perform. The marriage of modalities provides a whole new way of bringing healing, harmony and balance to the Earth and all beings.

In these times of war, food shortages, economic uncertainty, even the massive ecological disaster of climate change, people around the globe are faced with the task of growing beyond their comfort level in order to confront the vast unknowns that are arising in our world. We are so barraged with sights, sounds, information and persuasions that are frightening and seem beyond our ability to affect that there is a natural tendency to draw within and avoid all but the most certain information, focusing only on that which is before us or easily accomplished. If there is any certainty, however, it is that if ever there were a time for expanding our spiritual knowledge to encompass change, this is it. How do we do this? We look within, and we see how our brothers and sisters of the Earth, the plant and animal nations, accomplish growth to the unknown.

In sacred geometry, in order for a plant to decide how many leaves it must next produce, it looks at how much it has grown and then adds a proportional ratio.

Whether it decides to grow four leaves in a cluster or split into two stems and grow two leaves on each stem is given no clue beforehand as it rises from where it has been toward the light, reaching ever outward. But it is guided by a secret code held within it that is at the same time unique to that plant and shared with all plants like it and, as with all living things, incorporating a type of code that is shared.

Today we must look within to find that secret code, see where we have come from and where we must go. This quest for truth, knowledge, wisdom and growth can be a frightening journey. It requires that we reach toward a greater light and understanding only waiting for us to discover.

So, with this book, I am offering two 'knowns', Reiki and shamanism as currently practiced. Each is a viable healing modality; combined, they provide an entirely new level of spiritual insight and healing ability. The appellation of "Reiki Shaman," while new, could become a high attainment, with proficiency in both modalities.

This is the fourth in a series of books on environmental shamanism, a way of practicing shamanism that unites us with our surroundings, indeed, all of creation. Each of the first three books is a slice of healing, health and wholeness applied to the world, to create a trilogy of "people, places and things" in the shamanic way of viewing the world and all beings.[2]

This book takes the teachings of the first three books and applies the ancient Eastern art of Reiki, or "hands on" healing, to the mix. In essence, it takes shamanism and Reiki and combines them, so that all facets of people, places and things can find healing, health and wholeness through the blending of two strains of energy medicine. As we shall see, there really is no separation between them, Reiki itself is a form of shamanism.

Rather than limiting our approach of healing to "hands on," as Reiki has come to be understood, we will see that Reiki comes from the heart, head and hands via the energy body and, hence, can be applied near and far and out of body, anywhere in the world. We will carry forward our understanding of Reiki as shamanism by employing the energy body and through the shamanic journey applying Reiki long distance; and, as a form of shamanism, we will see that our journeys are inner and outer, exploring the universe that extends outside of ourselves as well as worlds within.

To become a Reiki shaman, one neither needs to be exceedingly proficient at shamanism, or Reiki. One does not need to be a Reiki master, for example. All it takes is some basic Reiki skills, and the basic shamanic skill: knowing how to journey shamanically.[3] Instructions on how to journey are included in the book, along with basic Reiki knowledge.

The book is divided into four chapters:

- The first provides a basis for understanding the energy body, or how we can do what we do by understanding who we truly are;

- The second outlines Reiki as a form of shamanism so that we might more fully incorporate that healing power instead of seeing Reiki as a separate modality of energy medicine;

- The third outlines shamanic journeying, which is the key to out-of-body healing, and how to incorporate Reiki with it;

- The fourth provides applications shared from personal experiences that may prove of use or value in exploring your own healing walk.

Included are instructions and exercises to develop capabilities for understanding the concepts, practicing and mastering them. Readers are encouraged to keep a notebook of their own observations that might prove useful in discovering new avenues for inner discovery; entries from my own notebook are provided as examples.

The first three chapters conclude with a short review of major points for easy reference, including key search words to find more material about related topics on the Internet. The fourth chapter includes a section on using quartz crystals that may be helpful in practicing Reiki shamanism, and a brief overview of some related healing modalities. The book concludes with a glossary of terms specific to doing healing work. In addition our Website, Healing the Earth/Ourselves, www.blueskywaters.com, offers books, CDs, tools, and additional reading material that may be ordered by mail or e-mail, as well as periodic classes and workshops.

If you absorb the information presented in these pages and practice the techniques described, you will change and your life will change. The way toward the light, following the secret inner code that leads us where we need to go, is beckoning! May many blessings unfold along your path! *Wisatologi Nihi!*

Now, let's get started.

Pathfinder Reiki Symbol

Problem Solver

Simplifies, moves to the next level by making the component parts of a seemingly unanswerable problem appear.

Chapter One

The Energy Body

*"The Sacred Hoop Of Life is larger than we
can see with our eyes or think with our
minds. Its completion resides in our hearts."*

— ASCENSION TESTS

The Western way of looking at the energetic body, or
energy body[1], is almost universal, and is perceived as
Eastern. But it is neither a universal way of looking at the
energy body, nor is it truly Eastern.

It was created by Westerners taking bits and pieces of
Eastern teachings and trying to make them conform to
Western mystical thought as part of the theosophical
movement of the late 19th and early 20th centuries.
Associated with Alice Bailey, it was set in stone, more or
less, with the publication of *The Chakras, a Monograph* by
C.W. Leadbeater, published by The Theosophical
Publishing House in 1927[2]), and with the publication of
a series of books by Sir John Woodroffe (1865–1936), also
known by his pseudonym Arthur Avalon (most notably
The Serpent Power, first published in 1919, which
translated Indian texts, including the *Sat-Cakra-
Nirupana,* written in 1577, and the *Padaka-Pancaka,*

containing descriptions of the centers and related practices, and *Gorakshashatakam,* which gives meditation techniques employing the chakras).[3]

The seven-chakra system has been attributed to earlier writers, such as H. P. Blavatsky, who founded the theosophical movement in the 19th century and wrote of chakras in her books, describing them based upon her own travels in India. It was not defined as a system such as the one we commonly see depicted today as going 1, 2, 3, etc, with all its various attributes, from the base or root chakra where one sits to the top of one's head, until Leadbeater popularized it. His book and Woodroffe's became the basis for later writers and thinkers who expanded on the concept, continuing to today.

The idea of seven chakras (the word itself is Sanskrit, meaning "wheels of light") comprising the energy body, with lesser chakras elsewhere, became established as the common Western way of looking at the energy body through the popularization of yoga in the 1950s and 1960s. Among its early proponents was Alan Watts, who was the author of 25 books focusing on Buddhism and its Zen variations, making "Eastern thought" popular in the US. He gave hundreds of lectures, influencing and being influenced by such opinion leaders as D.T. Suzuki, Aldous Huxley, Timothy Leary and Ram Dass. Among those who also adopted the seven-chakra system in the 1950s and helped make it the bedrock of modern energy body thought today was Dr. Randolph Stone, a chiropractor and osteopath, and founder of Polarity Therapy, which influenced dozens of energy modalities. Stone died at the age of 91 in 1981, and lectured well into his 70s, helping make the seven-chakra system even more firmly established in the most esoteric of energy body healing systems.

It's interesting today to read the works of those founders, Leadbeater, Woodroffe, Blavatsky, William Q. Judge and G. de Purucker, and how they differ from modern thought — particularly regarding yoga. For example, Blavatsky, Judge, and Purucker, devotees of Raja-yoga, were distrustful of chakras below the head as negative toward spiritual development. In her book *The Secret Doctrine,* Blavatsky calls use of the lower three chakras, which today are seen as grounding, and giving us vital contact with the Earth Mother, as being useful only in sorcery![4] Higher chakras were seen as good, lower chakras as bad. Today, if one viewed the energy body with such negativity, he or she would be seen at best as misguided for dissociating or negating life-sustaining energies. The efforts of these early writers to make Eastern Hindu and Buddhist concepts palatable and understandable to Westerners and complementary to Judeo-Christian belief systems infused their own prejudices, as well. This is true also of Reiki, though most Reiki practitioners are unaware of it.

Among many Native American peoples, the seven-chakra system appears incomprehensible, and rightly so. The idea of chakras is not an indigenous concept. Another way is to see the energy body as an energetic egg, as described in the works of Carlos Castaneda and Ken Eagle Feather, interpreting the teachings of Don Juan Matus.[5] In this way of seeing, the energy body has a luminescence with areas that are brighter, and lines going out from it that are cords that connect one to "reality." While certainly viable, it may not be the best analogy for describing how the energy body works for use in the energy medicine modalities discussed here.

In practice, the energy body can "look" like anything. In my own shamanic journeys, I don't "see" physical bodies, nor do I "see" the seven-chakra system; I see lines of energy, often in geometric shapes. Areas of light sometimes hold information that can be understood by "listening." (In the shamanic journey, our senses may be heightened so that the olfactory sense can tell more than visioning, much as a dog seems to "see" with its nose.) But, that is my way of perceiving, and there are many ways of perception. In essence, the chakras must be seen in context with the energy system or modality being described; for example, in Traditional Chinese Medicine, the chakras may be seen as energy centers along the meridians. In Eastern mysticism, they may be seen as gradations of consciousness. In the shamanic journey, they may be seen as locations for portals, or connections between the hard physical body and the lines of intention that connect, form, inform and direct energy in one's life (eg, connections through consciousness of one's family, friends, work, home, and former and past lives, that create a sacred geometry of physical "place," past, present and future).

A system described in the books of Drunvalo Melchizedek includes eight chakras that correspond to the musical scale.[6] It goes through the first three as base chakras, then goes through a half-step, or wall, to higher vibrations, then to the heart, then a change in polarity to the throat and the sixth at the eyes, but diverges to the seventh as the pituitary gland in the brain, where another half-step is contained before going through the crown to an eighth chakra which is the doorway to the next world. The Ancient Egyptian system had 13 chakras, including two heart chakras, with one for pure love and one for love relating to the body/emotions, which seems really quite advanced; it includes a chakra on the chin, which could be seen as presenting a face to the world; the nose, which is a directional point and can be seen as the focus of intent; and a pineal gland as a 45 degree angle between the third eye and crown. This system also corresponds to the musical scale, adding sharp notes.[7] Both the seven-chakra and 13-chakra and even a 22-chakra system are featured in various literatures, each with legitimate roots in the East and in ancient Egypt. The seven-chakra system is anything but written in stone!

Even among popular and accepted energy modalities there are differences in how the chakras work. The common understanding of chakras is based on ancient Indian Hindu Tantric esoteric traditions, loosely based on a model describing Kundalini as a Power that is said to "rise" upward from the base of the spine, touching the various chakras until reaching the crown, where it can unite with Divinity. In Traditional Chinese Medicine, chakra locations correspond to acupuncture points, and rather than Kundalini rising from the base chakra, the energy is seen as Qi and it is part of a circuit of energy called the Microcosmic Orbit, which comes up from the spine and back down the front of the body, entering at the *tan tiens* (the chakra below the navel) where it returns to the heart and loops back to the head.

Why Bother Over Chakras?

So, one might ask, if this seven-chakra system is nothing but an invented way of looking at the energy body and there are widely varying descriptions of it, with no real consensus, then why learn it? Easy: It works. Although the origins of the seven-chakra system could be seen as fanciful, as it has evolved it serves to explain quite a lot: it describes much that cannot be otherwise put into words, even if it is an imperfect model.

Nuclear physicists, for example, have descriptions, even diagrams of atoms, molecules and processes that don't accurately reflect the appearance of actual nuclear material. Consider, for example, the popular atomic symbol of a nucleus with the little spirals around it depicting electrons. The diagram is drawn so that the measurable effects, or uses, of atoms are roughly depicted. It's not meant to be a photograph of reality, just as the human chakra systems are not meant to be literal reality. In fact, it would be difficult to photograph an atom; most photos that show subatomic processes actually depict the energy released when one particle hits another creating an image of expended energy in the form of light on the film emulsion; but that in no way accurately depicts the appearance of a subatomic particle. Further, physicists today say atoms wink in and out of existence, and are considered to be both a wave and a particle, which defies common sense, or common notions of physical reality. But that's the reality of what is known of atoms, and the diagrams that scientists use are useful to create machines and processes that work, such as particle accelerators, clocks, even bombs, although the models themselves are "made up" and imperfect.

With that in mind, let's look at who we are, as physical and energetic beings, with bodies that are at the same time physical and energetic.

Basic Seven-Chakra Concepts

While the seven-chakra system has its flaws, it's important to know its basic parameters so as to be able to carry on conversations with fellow practitioners and others and to describe some of the effects of energy work. With this in mind, there are seven major chakras or power points in the human body that generally correspond with:

>*First chakra:* Root, Groin or base of the spine
>
>*Second chakra:* Sacral, abdomen; also called the Triple Warmer
>
>*Third chakra:* Navel or Solar Plexus
>
>*Fourth chakra:* Heart
>
>*Fifth chakra:* Throat
>
>*Sixth chakra:* Brow, Third Eye
>
>*Seventh chakra:* Crown, top of head

For those who can see the human aura, each has its own color and its own type of energy and each responds to a different musical key (vibration):

1st: Red – Grounding, security, primal energy

2nd: Orange – Relationships, emotions, sexuality, intimacy

3rd: Yellow – Energy, vitality, will power, personal authority

4th: Green – Balance, love, compassion, connection

5th: Blue – Communication, speech, expression, healing, creativity

6th: Indigo – Intuition, understanding, sixth sense, clairvoyance

7th: Violet – Enlightenment, transcendence, cosmic consciousness

Using the chakra system to explain behavior, dispositions and dis-ease (used here as being out of harmony; hence, ill) has been in common use since the last century, but, in recent years, the actual frequencies of the body have been scientifically measured. The human body is a veritable chatterbox of sound and electromagnetic vibration, with measurements of muscles ranging from zero to 250 cycles per second; brain waves operating at up to 20 cycles per second; the heart operating at about 225 cycles per second.

Each chakra has been measured at:

1. 640–800 Cycles per Second, or Hertz

2. 600–40 Hz

3. 400–600 Hz

4.   240–400 Hz

5.   100–240 (with a subwave at 800) Hz

6.   100–200, 740–900 Hz

7.   1100–1200 Hz[8]

It's important to note that nothing actually happens "in" a chakra; it is only a point of origin, where life energy is concentrated and released. Chakras are invisible to the human eye (except glimpsed or seen by adepts or spiritually trained individuals in shamanic journey or in meditative state), but as recent studies show they can be scientifically measured using sensitive instruments. In the terms of science, a chakra is "a unique electromagnetic wave generator" that creates a particular frequency.

Each of the chakras also responds to a note on the musical scale:

1 – G (below middle "C")
2 – D
3 – F
4 – G
5 – A
6 – D
7 – G

Sounds, when combined with intent, can produce miraculous effects in the body and mind (henceforth, the body/mind since they are inseparable in the energy body, though each has its unique characteristics), in conjunction with the chakras. For example, Tibetan

Buddhist meditators use *tingshas,* two small bells shaped like tiny cymbals. When they are rung together, each produces a slightly different tone. The tonal difference causes the bells to emit extremely low frequency sounds between 4 and 8 Hz, the range of brain waves that occurs during meditation (which also partially overlaps the rhythmic beating of shamanic drumming, from .8 to 5.0 Hz). Also, by meditating on the sound rhythms of our own hearts, we can access a powerful healing source.[9]

Scientists have documented the brain wave patterns that govern levels of consciousness:

Beta – The Beta brain wave pattern exists on the level of the conscious mind; starting at 14 cycles per second and usually averages about 21 cycles per second.

Alpha – The Alpha pattern exists on the level of the dreaming mind, during the creative state, and with minimal extra sensory perception (ESP) and cell energy renewal; it ranges from 7 to 14 cycles per second.

Theta – The Theta pattern activates a deeper state of ESP, and is the beginning level for psycho kinesis (PK); it ranges from 4 to 7 cycles per second.

Delta – The Delta pattern is usually recognized during deep sleep; during this time all ESP and PK events are stimulated and the qualities of total memory and total suggestibility are instilled; it ranges from 1/2 to 4 cycles per second.

The frequency for shamanic journeying through either a drum or rattle activates Theta waves in the brain, 4–7 cycles per second. Beating the drum or shaking the rattle about 180 times per minute accomplishes this. A faster cadence of 210 times per minute is used to "bring the shaman back" into ordinary reality.

The reason the drum is especially useful is that its unique sound has been scientifically proven to produce changes in the human central nervous system. It has several important effects:

- The rhythmic stimulation affects the electrical activity in the brain.

- A single beat of a drum contains many sound frequencies.

- The drumbeats are mainly low frequency, meaning more energy can be transmitted.

Native Americans have a simpler explanation of why the drum is so powerful. They say it has the same pulse as Mother Earth. They may be as close to the truth as the scientists. For scientists have measured the base resonant frequency of the Earth and it is indeed consistent with Native American drumming. The Earth's background base frequency, or "heartbeat," called Schumann resonance, has been rated at 7.8 cycles per second.[10] Indigenous peoples are among the most advanced on the face of the Earth in developing inner abilities of healing and understanding.[11]

Chakra Colors

Colors found in the chakras also mean a great deal to our physical/emotional/spiritual wellbeing, scientifically proven to impact our body and mind (which, seen as energetic systems can be seen as one: body/mind). When people are deprived a light frequency because their bodies cannot absorb it, they suffer from vitamin deficiencies, hormonal disorders, disturbances of the body's normal patterns, including sleep metabolic functions and depression.

The comfort zone of the human body includes light and heat, as well as soothing colors, so it is no coincidence that each of the chakras produces a natural color, or that our bodies respond to colors in the natural world. For example, green, the color of grass and growing things is a very soothing color, as is blue, the color of the clear sky. So is yellow, the golden shower of light emitted from our sun. Each is a soothing, invigorating color. And each is a natural color. No wonder people who work in artificial light all day can become irritable. Even the "whitest" white of artificial light is a dull yellowish red compared with the pure white of natural light. (Photographers know this, using "indoor" film designed to be more sensitive to the frequencies of artificial light for indoor photographs or using "hotter" or higher frequency lights to approximate sunlight). Yet our bodies emit pure, natural color all the time through the chakras.

Color is a perception of light. It's a challenge for some people to perceive color with the mind and hand, but our bodies produce it in vibrational form. The common denominator is that all is energy, everything, and hence all is vibration. While we refer to the vibration of light in wavelengths, rather than vibrations, it's a continuum: the sound spectrum we can perceive through our bodies in ordinary reality through our hearing sense ranges from 20 to 20,000 Hz; light vibrations range from 370 trillion to 750 trillion Hz.

All is energy, all is vibration, and we don't "see" everything around us, or even much of the vibrational information that is available. Consider "seeing with your own eyes" as an example. Visible light is only visible because we can see the source or the object that is being illuminated. The light itself cannot be seen, but is either seen as from the source or reflected; and that is further compromised by our inability to see the full spectrum. We can only perceive a narrow band of wavelengths. There are plenty of "colors" beyond those parameters, but we cannot see them, or see them as colors, but with proper equipment, they can be translated into vibrations that humans can perceive (infrared, ultraviolet light, x-rays) as light or into sound (microwave transmitting telephone and cell phone conversations; or seen as cooking food in the microwave oven). Because we can't see them with our eyes does not mean that they don't exist; the vibrations/wavelengths are there.

Further, our physical apparatus for translating vibration/frequency are biased by their limitations. White light isn't "white" but is the combination of all colors at once; black isn't "black" but an absence of light. Just as military night scopes translate absence of light as green, our minds could do the same. Our body/mind translates this smorgasbord of vibration/frequency, and filters, defines and makes sense of it, sometimes with only crude success. Yet, we deem this translated approximation as concrete certainty and call this "reality."

Body as Oscillator

Scientists have actually found that the body as a whole is an oscillator that vibrates at a measurable rate of 7 Hz; our atoms are calculated by scientists to vibrate at a much higher rate 10 (to the 15th power) Hz — in fact, a frequency too high to measure. Thoughts themselves have vibrational frequencies; some are high, some low. We intuitively know that when we are closest to Creator, to the Divine, our vibration rate is at its highest. But, until David R. Hawkins, measured the vibration rates of emotions, there was no scientific evidence for this.[12] Over 20 years Hawkins conducted experiments using kinesiology, or muscle testing, that demonstrated that the human body becomes stronger or weaker depending on a person's mental state. He developed a scale of 1–1,000 that maps human consciousness: 200 (or 20,000 cycles per second) and below weakens the body and from 200 to 1,000 makes the body stronger. Specifically, he measured rates for emotions, ie: Shame, 20; Guilt, 30; Apathy, 50; Grief, 75; Fear, 100; Desire, 125; Anger, 150; Pride, 175; Courage, 200.

Anything below 200 is destructive to life for both the individual and society at large; all levels above 200 are constructive expressions of power. The divine or enlightenment levels are in the 750–1,000 range. Above

200 are: Neutrality, 250; Willingness, 310; Acceptance, 350; Reason, 400; Love, 500; Joy, 540; Peace, 600.

Sadly, Hawkins concluded that 85 percent of the human race calibrates below the critical level of 200, while the overall average level of human consciousness was approximately 207.

Emotions Have Higher Frequencies

It's perfectly understandable that emotions are capable of a higher vibration rate than thoughts if you have ever noticed that emotions frequently are impossible to describe in words, since they are laden with a wealth of ideas and perceptions beyond the left brain's ability to process. Thinking (left-brain activity) occurs at the speed of reading; you "think" as fast as words form and are processed. But consciousness is at the speed of light, a much higher vibration. Hence, to access higher consciousness, emotions form a bridge — with the higher emotions blending with the lower levels of higher consciousness itself.

The right brain exists within this shadow world of emotion and symbolism that connects with higher consciousness, that mystics throughout the ages have accessed for wisdom, and healers touch through the Stillpoint, or the meditative state to "be here now," to bring higher energy into manifestation. While the left brain is plodding along trying to make sense of its surroundings and place in the world, the right brain (which sees in images and symbols) is holistically and immediately conscious of everything that it can process at that moment, at the speed of light itself. Plants and animals, not slowed down by words, logic, rationalizations and time sense, are closer to universal mind than are humans, but lack the sophisticated organizational ability of humans.[13]

All beings share Life Force (Ki)

Chakras are the Life Force (Ki) regulators in the human body and a person's health can be determined by how these areas of the body are balanced. But, just as the chakras can be used for personal healing, they also serve to show how each of us is intimately connected to the universe by the frequencies (the variations of those frequencies) in the universe.

The chakra field is called the "aura," a universal field extending several feet from a person that varies according to health, vibration rate of the chakras.

The power of the chakras is called Ki, or Life Force energy. Everyone is born with Ki and Ki is all around us. Our Ki goes up and down depending on our health and environmental factors. Since the human body receives, produces and transmits patterns of Life Force energy, as measurable through the chakras and in the aura, the human body can be seen as a pattern of energy, as well as an informational system. Thus, each second, a human body can be seen as an "event," a pattern of patterns with measurable frequencies (just as rocks, trees, other "matter" can also be seen as "events"), constantly pulsating and constantly changing — although they appear static and unchanging to the human eye as "frozen light," an "event" in vibration viewed at one moment in time, unless one is in an altered state brought on by meditation, shamanic journeying, vision quest, fasting, sweat lodge, drug inducements or other activities visionaries have used throughout the centuries to perceive what is really "real."[14]

We believe everything around us is "real" because we can see or touch it, though this is not totally the case. We touch, see or feel the "event" of the thing we touch, see or feel, not the thing itself, which is always in process. Just as scientists say that matter pulses in and out of existence, and all matter is both a wave and a particle, nothing is truly "here" all the time. It is through these pulsations of Life Force energy that we project ourselves into the universe. We each create around us this aura, a "prayer field," that is our current state of emotion, health, intent, our very "being" in a constant information field that connects us with everything around us and the universe.

How? Consider each of these chakras as tiny, powerful radio transmitters broadcasting these levels of our being; together, making an overall pattern, or message. With that prayer field, we are constantly sending out into the universe our thoughts, perceptions, orientations and beliefs and are literally creating our reality. In shamanic terms, we are constantly adjusting our "assemblage points," the areas in energy body that "connect" us to what we perceive as reality, both with our senses, and beyond our senses, to ground us into a reality we can perceive and understand. Properly speaking, the energy body exists beyond the physical plane; in humans, such a body extends twenty-seven feet in each direction and thereafter continues into other dimensions. It can be described as a star tetrahedron, in sacred geometry, with lines (invisible in ordinary reality) that extend out into time and space.[15] Indeed, it is by following these invisible lines, or cords, that we travel in a shamanic journey.

The way of the universe, whether seen by a medicine man or a physicist is the same: all is energy, patterns of energy, whether appearing in particle or wave or subtle energy we cannot measure. Thought is energy. Intent is energy. Trees, rocks and grass are energy. Prayer is energy, too. We each are a part of this holographic universe, where everything is connected, and what we do affects everything, even if we don't give our actions, thoughts, behaviors much attention. It is all a Great Mystery, and all beings are part of it, part of the great sacred Hoop of Life.

Exercise 1 Your Energy Body as a Medicine Wheel

Consider yourself for a moment, feeling your physical body. If it helps, look at yourself in a full-length mirror. Your physical body is the densest form of your body, but it is, by no means, the extent of your body.

If you put your feet apart slightly and extend your arms straight out from your body (as in the famous Leonardo da Vinci drawing *Vitruvian Man*), you will see that your form describes a perfect circle. If you look around you, turning completely around, you will see that the world as you see it describes a perfect circle. This is the medicine wheel that is you. In native way, we call things that have power "medicine," the power of the thing itself, its essential nature. Your medicine is your essential nature, your past, present and future extending into time and space. This is accomplished through your energy body. In Western way, we describe chakras as being power centers in the body; accretions of power that have measurable qualities and characteristics. Whether we follow the seven-chakra model or "see" another one, our bodies do have areas of greater power that can be seen shamanically or in nonordinary reality.

You do not need to take drugs to "see" in nonordinary reality; all the chemicals necessary are already in the brain. It only takes learning a few techniques, such as journeying through shamanic drumming. You may see yourself in this way as a line of chakras, in the seven-chakra system, as a luminous egg with brighter areas inside it, or another way, in accordance with your own view or dream of the world.

Another way to visualize how we are energetically put together is to, with your arms still straight out to your sides in front of the mirror, imagine that the straight arms out form a straight line across your shoulders; now push this imaginary line down a little bit so that it is even with your chest. Now see your legs as a point. See two inverted pyramids, one with the flat base even with your chest, pointing down; the other even with your knees, pointing up. That is a star tetrahedron. From each of these points, radiating outward, are lines of energy that go out through time and space.[16]

Whichever way you see yourself, remember that your chakras, or energy centers, are also located outside your physical body, too.

Regardless of the seven-chakra model, we live in a 3-D world and are connected with all-time, no-time, or what is "really real," that is, dimensions beyond this one, too. So, there really are two more chakras:

1) Beneath your feet, that grounds and connects you to the Earth Mother, and

2) One above your crown that acts as a doorway for other dimensions. This above or "eighth" chakra is developed by practicing Reiki or other high vibration healing modalities or techniques. Indeed, it is through the attunement process in Reiki, and implanting symbols in the energy body, that this chakra is grown. Although the "new" chakra, that of super consciousness or Christ consciousness, or connecting with the Plume of Quetzalcoatl, always exists in potential if not in limited fashion for anyone, the attunements seem to open up this chakra just as the attunements make normally minor chakras in the palms fully opened, equal or almost equal to the power-emitting ability of the other "major" chakras. This "super" chakra is developed in its greatest capacity through the second and third (Reiki Master) attunements.

Continue to look at yourself in the mirror. Regardless of your internal dialogue, such as "I'm fat" or "I'm beautiful," "I'm short" or "I'm tall," you are far more than the sum of your self-talk, or your physical body.

You are immortal; your body is only here for a short time. You are a child of Creator and the Earth Mother, a miracle, a walking rainbow of colors, vibrations. As Children of Earth and Sky, it is our challenge to bring love and light to the Earth.

Aho.

From the Energy Notebook: Who Is This Seven-Chakra Guy?

When I was growing up, in the 1950s, I had an ability — at the time I thought it was a curse — to be able to accurately dream of events before they happened and "see" things that others told me weren't there. It made for some embarrassing moments, since it was not a socially acceptable or well understood phenomena in my cultural milieu. I tried to repress it, ignore it, and pretend it didn't exist.

But I cannot forget the first time I saw a drawing of the seven-chakra system. It showed the common depiction of a Buddha-like figure, seated in the Lotus position, with hands holding fingers together (mudras), and the seven, colored, glowing circles of light (chakras). The wheels of light went from the base of the spine, to the abdomen (the much caricatured, "stare into your navel"), the solar plexus, the heart, the throat, the "third eye," between the eyes and the crown.

I thought: "Who is this guy?"

It didn't look like anything I had "seen" — either in glimpses in waking life or in Dreamtime. People told me it was "Eastern" and Buddhist, and that was some kind of esoteric knowledge. I thought, "It doesn't look natural." And so, for years, I walked around thinking that East Asians had different energy systems than we in the West did.

When I discovered that the seven-chakra system was only a model, that the energy body can and does look different to individuals, and constantly changes, it made immediate sense to me. In short, I trusted what I saw, not what someone told me I should be seeing. That has been my guide since that "Aha!" moment: *Trust what you see, not what someone tells you to see.* Of course, read and learn about other ways of seeing and systems of viewing shamanically, but let those systems be as lenses to try on — like trying on pairs of sunglasses until you find the right fit — and discard those that don't work. Understand that they do work for others, and are valid, but trust your senses. See what you see!

In this light, be aware, also, that if you practice Reiki, you will "grow" chakras. First, the attunement process itself implants symbols in the energy body that causes a so called "eighth" chakra to "grow" above the crown chakra, that each succeeding attunement will help to develop it, and second, your so-called "secondary" chakras in the palms will also develop.

Several years ago, a person in India studying long-distance viewing had seen some of my writings and sought permission to view me energetically. Sure, I said, as long as what was seen was reported. The student wrote back that what was seen couldn't possibly be true because I had "unusually large" chakras in the hands, that appeared to be major chakras, not minor ones. I wrote back, in great glee, that I was a Reiki master with a thriving practice, hence, the palm chakras, having healing energy passing through them regularly had grown to accommodate the transmission of energy.

Our chakra system is mutable; our energy body cannot conform to a static depiction or preconceived notion. Our energy bodies are living, adapting systems of energy.

Review

Exploring the energy body and the chakras:

- Understand that the energy body extends beyond the physical body into other dimensions of time and space, connecting with everything else in the holographic universe.

- Appreciate that our physical senses are limited but that doesn't mean that whole realms don't exist outside of what we perceive as our "ordinary" reality.

- Understand that the seven-chakra system for describing the energy body is crude and approximate and that other descriptions are equally valid, or moreso, depending on how it is used.

- See yourself as a medicine wheel, connecting above with below and yourself as the center in this world.

Internet key words: *chakra, energy body, star tetrahedron, MerKaBa, vibrational medicine, energy medicine.*

Pathfinder Reiki Symbol

Stillpoint

Chapter Two

Reiki as Shamanism

"The true test of a religion is not what you believe, but what you do."

— Ascension Tests

Millions of people around the world have been exposed to the now well substantiated healing power of Reiki. Most are aware that it has its origins in Japan, but may not know that much of what is taught about Reiki in the West regarding its most basic premises, processes and even treatment has been misrepresented — even the most widespread accounts of its founder, Dr. Mikao Usui.[1] It should not be hidden any longer, cannot be dismissed, and should not be hushed up as a secret: Dr. Usui was a shaman, Reiki's origins are shamanic, and by any measure, Reiki is a form of shamanism.

In the literature are contrary accounts over whether Dr. Usui was a Christian or a Buddhist. It was said that he was trying to discover how to heal with the hands as Christ did. To be sure, it is said that Jesus taught His disciples how to use this healing power and it is shown in The Dead Sea Scrolls that the Essenes used techniques similar to Reiki.[2] In fact, symbols and ideas associated with Reiki can be traced back to several hundred years before Christ's birth.[3] The Buddhist origins of Reiki can also hardly be overlooked. Parallels exist between the Kurama-Koyo Buddhist symbols and philosophy and Reiki, and it is believed that Dr. Usui had studied at a young age at a monastery of Tendai Buddhism (one of the very few photographs of him shows him in either a Zen or Taoist robe). The Buddhist symbols may have their origins in Hindu Ayurvedic medicine with offshoots in ancient Egypt.[4] It also has interesting parallels in Native American cultures.[5]

In Tibetan Buddhism, the healing effects seen with Reiki were said to be a common outgrowth of higher levels of mind/body training. But, since dis-ease was seen as karmic, actually using the healing power was deemed inconsequential, perhaps even detrimental, to a personal path of enlightenment. In other words: Why use healing power on another when it is that person's karmic disposition to be ill? In fact the first known reference in Japan to what would become Reiki is by Mong Dsi, around 300 BC, in a paper complaining that too many monasteries were focusing on worldly purposes and not properly using the symbol, then called Ling Qi, for connection with the divine nature.[6] In this sense, Dr. Usui would seem to be going against his Buddhist training. Although these symbols, or similar ones were well known in ancient Buddhist texts, to use them in any other way than to achieve enlightenment or Nirvana to end Samsara, the perpetual cycle of birth and death, would be seen as a form of attachment to the world that is antithetical to Buddhist thought. This is not to say that one cannot be Buddhist and practice shamanism, or Reiki Shamanism; quite the contrary! It is the purpose of anyone who pursues a healing path, or path to enlightenment, to change him or herself in a way that is of benefit to all living beings, and not only the "self." Such a transformation is intrinsic to "enlightenment," and the path that leads to it is called the "Path of the Bodhisattva," or the way of compassionate service. In this sense, the creation of Reiki is both Buddhist and shamanic.

Since the discovery of his early writings, it becomes clear that Dr. Usui was indeed a follower of Buddhism, but he was also a believer in various shamanic concepts, and he practiced shamanic techniques.

He was born on August 15, 1865, in the Kyoto district of Japan, in the province of Gifu. He began his practice around 1920, opening a clinic in Tokyo in 1921. He apparently trained about 2,000 people in Reiki and his fame spread, enough so that he moved to a larger house in 1925, and he died March 9, 1926.[7] A reading of his early published works, his personal manual and other writings and the recollections of those who knew him, gives a different picture than was originally shown in the West. For example, it's obvious now that he was not a Christian, and certainly was not a Christian missionary; he did not teach at Doshisha University in Kyoto and no document has ever been found that supports the claim that he attended the University of Chicago.[8]

These were all stories told about him by Mrs. Hawayo Takata, a student of Chujiro Hayashi, who was a student of Dr. Usui, and brought Reiki to Hawaii in 1937. She established several clinics and became associated with the teaching of Reiki in the West. It could very well be that in the days before and after World War II, Mrs. Takata sought to distance the healing method she was teaching from Japan, and make it more palatable to Western, Christian ideas. Her method of teaching became known as "traditional" Reiki, but it was anything but traditional, as Dr. Usui's own notebook suggests.[9] Dr. Usui's methods are deeper in their roots than modern interpretations, and much broader than previously thought.

Foremost, in his manuals and published statements, Dr. Usui called Reiki an original therapy built upon the power of the universe. In Japanese, it is not considered a *shinko ryoho* (religious therapy) but a *shinrei ryoho* (a spiritual method of healing). Further, in Dr. Usui's own words, it is a path of spirit, *kokoro,* which means mind and heart blended as one. These are shamanic characteristics, albeit shared with other spiritual traditions.

The way in which people are treated using the hands, not for physical manipulation, but for guiding energy, transmitting energy, breaking energetic blockages and removing spiritual intrusions, is most definitely shamanic and demonstrated in other cultures, including Native American (see my previous book, *Finding Sanctuary in Nature: Simple Ceremonies in the Native American Tradition for Healing Yourself and Others).* It is intuitive, rather than the set hand placements or prescribed movements taught by Mrs. Takata. Traditional indigenous medicine men and women across the north and central American continent perform similar intuitive healing, all shamanic acts down to the hand gestures outlined in Dr. Usui's notebook.[10]

The story of how Dr. Usui received Reiki is consistent with indigenous pathways for acquiring shamanic skills or knowledge, as well. He recounts it in his written works, saying simply "I was inspired." In fact, he prepared himself for a mountaintop fast on Mt. Kurama, which is today about a 20-minute train ride from the old capital of Kyoto. He is said to have taken 21 stones with him so that he would know how many days had passed. After 21 days he felt an energy come down through the top of his crown. But it wasn't until he came down from the mountaintop and miraculously cured several people did he realize what had happened. The symbols that are taught today are those that came, written in the ancient Japanese Kanji form of writing.

This method of fasting, even using stones, is an ancient and traditional method for finding enlightenment among most cultures. In Tibetan Buddhism, for example, followers of Buddha will attempt to touch the *bardo* (the intermediate state following death) in normal awareness through calling up inner symbols and spiritual forces through *tho-dol* or *thos-grol,* or "liberation by hearing." It is said that only one who "prepares to hear" can hear the call for liberation, or develop sufficient inner vision to see the Great Perfection (*rdzogs-chen,* or Sanskrit: *sampannakrama*), and achieve the state of perfection, which is perceived through perfect integration. In this process, which can employ extensive meditation, including fasting in remote places, it's not unusual to receive symbols through inspiration. These picture-symbols are often seen as part of the Great Symbol *(phyag-rgya chen-po,* or Sanskrit: *mahamudra),* the great attitude of unification and wholeness.

By incorporating these symbols in a "do" or path (or *tao* in Chinese), with Reiki, or creating a *Reiki-do,* Dr. Usui was leading a way of health and wholeness that was the direct result of his fast. This is a traditional Native American way of finding one's self and bringing that gift into the world, as well. Buddhism dovetails beautifully with Native American concepts, beliefs and ideals, as you can see. Ven. Dhyani Ywahoo, chief of the Green Mountain Ani Yunwiwa (Cherokee), is founder and spiritual director of Sunray. It is a Tibetan Buddhist Dharma center with a teaching facility, stupa and nunnery in Bristol, Vt. She successfully combines Buddhism with the ancient Ywahoo (Cherokee: Great Mystery) lineage of spiritual teachings. Her name, Dhyani, denotes her Tibetan Buddhist teachings, referring to The Five Dhyani Buddha's, or Great Buddha's of Wisdom. Each Buddha is believed to be capable of overcoming a particular evil with a particular good, and each has a complete system of symbolism, which coincidentally (there are no coincidences!) corresponds to colors of the medicine wheel. Each direction is a Power that can be accessed for greater knowledge and understanding, and is explored in my book *Finding Sanctuary in Nature: Simple Ceremonies in the Native American Tradition for Healing Yourself and Others.*

In Native America, the pipe fast, or vision quest, has been a mainstay among various tribes, practiced in various ways, from the four-day fast popularized as Lakota (though it's not as uniform as many may think) to the Cherokee *us'ste'lisk* (being alone with a sacred fire for a variable period of days).[11] This method of learning to "see" what is "really real" is essentially shamanic, and is perfectly described as *kokoro,* in Dr. Usui's words, "mind and heart blended as one."

The very name Rei-Ki, that Dr. Usui gave his method of healing is indicative of more than has been widely promulgated in the West. In Japanese, the character Rei stands for mystery, gift, holy, and nature spirit, or invisible spirit; Ki means Life-Force energy. Rei-ki has been defined as "Guided Life-Force Energy," or healing energy that has wisdom, guided by Spirit. It is universal. As William Lee Rand, founder of the International Center for Reiki Training, says: "Reiki is Ki guided directly by the higher power, also known as God, the Supreme Being, The Universe, The Universal Mind, All That Is, Jehovah, Krishna, Buddha, The Great Spirit, etc."[12] So, it is universal in its origin and application, spiritual, not religious — or, in Dr. Usui's words, *shinrei ryoho,* not a *shinko ryoho.* This, again, is shamanic in nature.

Dr. Usui's *Reiki-do,* or path for using these symbols, is noteworthy for its roots and practice. Reiki by its nature is counter to the Buddhist premise of not interfering in the life path of another, in that by helping to release negative thoughts, feelings, memories, associations and to reprogram one's outlook, even being, it balances and shifts karma. To the traditional Buddhist way of thinking, it is not illness or dis-ease that is the problem, but the state of mind while experiencing suffering. Taking an active approach toward healing could be seen as having serious consequences for several lifetimes, interposing one's self in the working out of karma, and altering the karmic balance following from the healing and resulting changed life path.

This healing approach, or in Cherokee, *duyuktv* (Doo-*Yook*-Tuh), or *way* of harmony and balance, is essentially a proactive force toward wholeness. To walk in peace and harmony (Cherokee, or Tsalagi: *aisv nvwhetoheyada alenvwedoheyadv)* is both a blessing and a way of being that is centered in conscious choices, or personal responsibility as an active agent in the world. This choice to be in harmony (Navajo, or Dine: *hozho)* as an active principle and at oneness with the universe, is both essentially Native American and ultimately shamanic, as it calls upon Powers greater than ourselves to guide, help and achieve.

This process of unfoldment of creative power, or creation of reality, is not without antecedents in Buddhism; it is the crystallization of meditation as a process of creation *(sristi-krama, utpranna-krama,* or in Tibetan: *bskyed-rim)*. However, it is more aligned with the shamanic tradition of Tibet, called *Bön,* which is an ancient shamanic spiritual practice thousands of years older than Buddhism. It has been largely absorbed into Tibetan Buddhism and survives in many rituals, initiations, meditations, and deities. It may be here that Dr. Usui diverged from his Buddhist training, forsaking the monastery for an active healing practice. For, although ancient Buddhism contains the origins of some Reiki symbols, it is through the shamanic experience of fasting, honoring a sacred place, receiving a vision and actively forging a visioned path (dancing the dream) in harmony with the Powers that Dr. Usui transformed Buddhist thought into shamanic practice. It has been noted by others that Reiki has clear ties to Qigong, a method of connecting the self to universal energy, and

Shintoism. Qigong also has strong shamanic roots: it's believed to have originated from the dances of early Wu Shaman. Dance was used in their ceremonies to induce trance states for communicating with the spirit world, including dancing their totems or power animals, wearing of skins and masks. Shintoism derives from the Yayoi culture, which originated in the island of Kyushu around the 2nd century BC. They practiced agricultural rites and shamanism, led by shamans (called *miko* — the same as in Native American Choctaw *"miko,"* or Chickasaw, *minko,* often spelled *mingo,* that means "leader" or chief — that today in Japan *means* "shrine maiden; virgin consecrated to a deity" who serves Shinto shrines). These shamans evolved into religious leaders in what came to be a Shinto-Buddhist amalgamation, that later merged with Confucianism. During the period in which Dr. Usui lived, this religious system with shamanic roots had a strong connection with a resurrected Shinto belief structure that included *musubi* (the mystical power of *becoming* or of *creation,* the same Power that many Native American songs celebrate, called *niyan* in Lakota, or wind, or the force of change that propels intent through the use of Tibetan prayer flags).[13] This belief was combined with absolute faith and respect for the Imperial line, which Dr. Usui embodied in his writings, dedicating his works to the Emperor and quoting him extensively. Shintoism at that time was also evolving into an outward expression and an inward belief structure (two forms: Shrine Shinto or *Jinja* and Sect Shinto or *Kyoha*).

A central Shinto belief at the time Dr. Usui lived is also at its heart shamanic: the creating and harmonizing power *(musubi)* of *kami* and the way of truth through *kami (makoto)*. The way of *kami* is not through a written doctrine, but through belief, and great truths are given through the forces of nature, including clouds, trees, winds, even unusual land formations. (For more on the power of land forms and their divine nature, including geomancy and the origins of feng shui, see my previous book, *Clearing: A Guide to Liberating Energies Trapped in Buildings and Lands).* It is through visiting, meditating and visioning at holy places, that one receives truth, and it can include being possessed by an animal (shamanic power animals). Although Dr. Usui does not explicitly refer to any animals or a *kami* belief, in the few writings of his that remain, the fact that he would take a 21-day fast at a recognized holy place and come down from the mountain with a new truth *(makato),* along with his written words expressing the Shinto belief in Imperial power and obvious spiritual adherence to vision as a source of truth and way of harmony (recognizing *musubi),* speaks to this belief that is shamanic by definition and history.

Finally, if there is any doubt as to the shamanic origins, intent and application of *Reiki-do* as a system, or Dr. Usui as a shamanic practitioner as its originator, one has only to look to the last evidence of the master himself: the Kanji emblem representing the word "Reiki" as carved on Dr. Usui's memorial stone itself.[14] As illustrated opposite, the symbol for Reiki can be broken down into its component parts with: the bottom, the wavy lines representing Ki, or Life-Force Energy, as mist; the top with an umbrella shape and horizontal lines are falling; the middle, which is the key component. In this

Symbols on Dr. Usui's grave

depiction, the three box shapes are the mouths of people upturned and open in awe, as the mist, bottom Ki, is transformed into rain, top. In the center, the T shape with the two inverted Vs, is the central message: shaman. Together, the symbol for Reiki, which is on Dr. Usui's grave and reproduced all over the world in various forms is essentially the same, with very few people actually knowing what it means. It says: Shaman Who Makes Rain. The word "Rei" as expressed by this symbol, means "rainmaker."[15] The mist can be seen as the Life Force Energy in its potential or unrealized state. The rain is brought forth by one who can see Spirit, and allow this miracle to happen, even as people stare in awe (or alternatively, with mouths open to receive or be nourished by the spiritual replenishment and benefits) for bringing Ling (rain), healing, nourishing physical manifestation, from Ki (mist).

Dr. Usui's memorial stone itself relates his experience as going to the mountain Kuramayama to start an asceticism, or *shyu gyo,* meditation and fasting, and "on the beginning of the 21st day, suddenly he felt one large Reiki over his head (the symbol) and he comprehended the truth. At that moment he got Reiki," or *Ryoho,* meaning ancestral remedy or therapy. This Kanji on the Usui Memorial at Saihoji Temple, Tokyo, pretty much says it all. It was erected in February 1927, and was written by Admiral Ushida, Dr. Usui's successor as head of the Reiki Society in Japan.

In short, the available literature, the verified facts, even the inscription on his memorial confirms an inescapable fact: Dr. Usui's practice was shamanic in origin and application, even in its description for the

Reihou or spiritual method, Reiki method, he founded: *Shaman Who Makes Rain.*

Let no one say that Reiki and shamanism are not kindred modalities. Indeed, they are one, and now can be taught as intended.

The Key to Reiki is Ki

Reiki has been called the lazy person's Qigong, because it does not require years of study or painstaking training. Reiki is a gift from Creator that requires no training in its use, but is acquired, like grace in Judeo/Christian culture, as a benefit for humankind. It is not religious, but fits well with all religions, and is finding increasing popularity among Christians, who delight in finding a new way to express compassion toward others and relieve suffering while at the same time creating a closer connection with God.[16] This ease of acquiring proficiency has helped make it popular in the West. A tremendous amount of knowledge is not required to learn or practice Reiki; indeed, Reiki I, the first attunement, requires little if any thought, and no knowledge of the symbols. Only the transmission of Reiki to others requires knowledge, understanding and proficiency.

Reiki is passed on by attunements, that is the direct implanting of the symbols first seen by Dr. Usui in his moment of apprehending them and being attuned to them on the mountain. Every person who practices Reiki has a lineage extending, by personal attunement, from one Reiki Master to another, from Dr. Usui to the present day. It matters not how close one is to Dr. Usui — whether, say, sixth generation or 20th generation, the power is the same. For example, my own Reiki lineage through the Karuna Reiki® I practice is: Mikao Usui: Hawayo Takata: Bethal Phaigh: William Lee Rand (Karuna Reiki®): Jim PathFinder Ewing.

Some people may mistakenly think they are practicing Reiki by using hands-on healing techniques, or by simply focusing on the symbols, but it requires an attunement by a Reiki Master to implant the symbols in order for them to work.

Once attuned, one is able to practice Reiki, with the Reiki energy passing through the hands and other chakras. It will often just "turn on," whether one is consciously aware of it or not. Focusing on the Reiki energy will cause it to flow, as well. While the sensation of "hot hands" is often associated with Reiki "turning on," that's not always the case. There may be a tingling sensation in the hands, and even cold hands with no apparent sensation. The Reiki energy is still being transmitted, even when no discernable sensation is perceived — and is also being transmitted by chakras in the feet, brow, heart, etc. The Reiki sensation in the hands is most noticeable because the hands are most often used to direct Reiki energy and most obviously describe the act of a Reiki treatment; that is, holding the hands toward the patient or person to be healed. But Reiki can "turn on" at any time, and does, with little or no prompting, or totally on its own, going wherever it is needed. Have faith, and enjoy the ride.

It's possible that one could fast for a number of days or perform other ascetic rituals to obtain the symbols, or others. Healing with the hands is not limited to Reiki; for example, using the Powers, or stones, and even Earth energy, can be used for powerful ceremonies and healing — even at a distance.[17] But obtaining an attunement by a Reiki Master is simple, and with the profusion of Reiki practitioners worldwide, easy to accomplish. Everything about Reiki is easy and simple and available.

The key to Reiki is: Ki. It could be called the body/mind's secret weapon for health and healing. Why? Because Life Force Energy is all around us. It is available to everyone, within every "thing," abundant, omnipresent, ever flowing and only limited by one's ability to consciously use it. That's the "Ki" part of Reiki. It is utterly abundant.

The other part, using it to heal is available to everyone, too. Every human being has a natural ability to heal self and others. But it must be "turned on," as with switches, for it is locked within the DNA.

Since the Reiki power has its own wisdom and goes directly where healing is needed, the person who transmits the Reiki energy does not control the healing effect. As in most forms of shamanism, the Reiki practitioner is the "hollow bone" allowing the Reiki guides (spiritual beings) to direct the healing energy as it is needed — including the person performing the Reiki treatment. As one heals, the person doing the healing is also healed, as the Reiki power passes through the Reiki practitioner.[18] Hospitals across America are recognizing the benefits of Reiki training even if they don't fully understand exactly how it works and some states offer education credits for nurses learning the techniques.[19] Reiki training is actually recommended by some hospitals for those who work in their critical and intensive care units. But it is not limited to people in the health professions. Anyone can receive Reiki treatments, and anyone can learn it and use it in daily life.

Reiki healing ability is within every human being only awaiting attunement from a Reiki Master. There commonly are three levels of Reiki as taught in America:

- Reiki I, whereby the practitioner can heal self and others.

- Reiki II, which adds long-distance healing and other techniques.

- Reiki III, the Reiki Master level, whereby attunements may be passed on to others.

Different Reiki teachers modify the teachings somewhat, but they all derive from the Reiki technique discovered by Dr. Usui. It was kept as a closely-guarded system until the mid-1980s and the fees for the master level of training were quite high. For example, it is said that Mrs. Takata didn't begin initiating Reiki Masters (who are able to teach and make the necessary chakra attunement on others) until 1970 and for that she charged $10,000. Iris Ishikura, one of Mrs. Takata's Reiki Masters, began charging a more reasonable fee and her Reiki Masters charged less as well, making it more available to more people here in the West. Today, probably the most well-known organization teaching Reiki is the International Center for Reiki Training in Southfield, Mich., founded by Reiki Master William Lee Rand.[20]

Reiki is spiritual in nature, but it is not a religion. Because Reiki comes from God, many people find that using Reiki puts them more in touch with the experience of their religion. The Reiki power is sacred, however, and should be treated with respect. Although it can only be used for good, its power is life-changing.

The three main Reiki symbols are:

- Cho ku Rei (Show-Koo-Ray), which is the power symbol, used to "power up" a Reiki practitioner or focus the Reiki power upon a person or object.

- Sei he ki (Say-Hey-Kee), which is the mental/emotional symbol, used to bring harmony to any person or situation and is especially used in healing practice.

- Hon sha ze sho nen (Hahn-Shay-zee-show-non, or Hon-Shay-Zee for short), which is the distance healing symbol, used to heal persons and situations across the room, across town, across the continent or on the other side of the planet (including Earth healing generally) and can be applied to karmic matters. It means, "no past, no present, no future" and transcends time and space. It can also be used as a "bank" for holding Reiki to be dispensed to the person over time. For example, when working from home long distance on someone in a hospital, I might put the symbol over the person with the intent while working to "power it up" so that it works as a time-release mechanism after the session is over to give the patient the amount of Reiki continuously needed over the next two or three weeks.

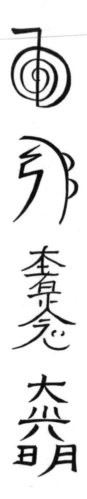

Usui Reiki Symbols:
Choiku-Rei, Sei Heki, Hon Sha Ze Sho Nen, and Dai Ko Myo

The Master Reiki symbols, which include the Usui Dai Ko Myo (Die-Koh-Me-Oh) and the Tibetan Dai Ko Mio, can help access life purpose or destiny. The Tibetan Fire Serpent figure is used to align the chakras preparatory to an attunement.

In addition to these symbols, similar to Dr. Usui's experience on the mountain, I have found in Dreamtime four other symbols that are useful, that may be called the PathFinder Symbols:

1. *The Problem Solver* – Simplifies, moves to the next level by making component parts of a seemingly un-answerable problem appear.

2. *Stillpoint* – Balance, centeredness, doorway.

3. *Threshold/Ascension* – Two symbols, active and done: beginning/end, passing through/completion.

Since these symbols came to me in 2002, I have shared them with other Reiki masters to see if they work for them. In each case, they have worked well, even without a hands-on attunement with them.

There are other symbols that various modalities use, as well. For example, Karuna Reiki®, which employs the Tibetan/Usui symbols depicted also includes eight additional symbols, plus the Om symbol. The Om symbol is a powerful one for accessing creation vibration, calming and becoming one with the Flow of Creation. In Jo Ki Kei Shin Reiki, formerly called Johrei Reiki, two symbols are employed, including the Antakarana and the Jo Ki Kei Shin symbol. The

Antakarana is an ancient and powerful distance healing symbol that can help bring harmony to any situation. [21] The Jo Ki Kei Shin symbol is a straight-line, white energy that can blast away disharmonies in the auric field and remove spiritual intrusions; it is employed by the practitioner sitting directly opposite the client in a straight-backed chair and focusing on the symbol. The client will often feel disoriented, or may have a perception of extreme lucidity. (Although I don't normally refer to people who come to me as "clients," preferring to think of them, and relate to them, as the individuals who come to me, in writing this book, it's less cumbersome to say "client.")

Most of the symbols are, again, only useful if implanted in the aura through the attunement process; but the three PathFinder symbols and Antakarana can be used by anyone; simply draw one on a card or piece of paper and place it next to your bed at night or under your pillow for a few nights. Results may be subtle or dramatic. Often, help will come in Dreamtime, so that you may sort through the issue yourself. The Antakarana is useful anytime, anywhere and can be used simply as a design put somewhere in a room, even on a refrigerator to keep in the consciousness, so that healing/ harmonious energies may be kept close at hand or subtly operating in the area; the same is true of the Om symbol.

A Typical Reiki Attunement

A typical Reiki attunement for Reiki I consists of a Reiki Master following a few simple steps while the student sits fully clothed and in a relaxed state in a chair. They may include reading an outlining explaining Reiki power, a short guided meditation, and then implanting (or blowing) the symbols into the chakras of the crown and hands. These steps may vary from Reiki teacher or Reiki tradition, but they are very common. The entire process usually takes no more than 30 minutes.

A Typical Reiki Treatment

A typical Reiki treatment consists of a practitioner using a set of hand placements on or near the body of the client. The hand placements can be part of a full body healing session or just certain hand placements to treat a specific area of the body. The Reiki practitioner may not even actually touch the client, or only momentarily. The client is fully clothed and usually is lying down, preferably on a massage table, but a low bed or cushions on the floor will do.

The symbols can be used for purposes other than healing. For example, *Sei he ki* can be incorporated into a person's auric field to act as a way to protect the individual. With meditation and intent, the symbol will automatically "turn on" whenever a negative thought is directed at the practitioner no matter what he or she may be doing. In large crowds it will automatically "turn on" to protect negative thought forms from lodging in the auric body.[22] For example, frequently while in the parking lot before entering a shopping mall or grocery or department store, I'll stop for just a moment and say "Shields up, Scotty!" — referring to the old *Star Trek* TV episodes — allowing myself to imagine invisible shields with *Sei he ki* symbols on them going up to protect me all around.

In each case, whatever negative energy is encountered will be mirrored back to the sender, transmuted into healing energy to help that person with his or her issues. As mentioned earlier, once a person has an attunement, Reiki energy will automatically "turn on" whenever and wherever it's needed. It's remarkable to walk into a crowded place and see the "lights turn on" in people's eyes as this symbol becomes unconsciously activated.

The power symbol, *Cho ku Rei,* can also be used to empower an individual in difficult situations, accessing the knowledge to lead one out of a jam. All one has to do is focus on the symbol *Cho ku Rei* or use the words as a mantra and the "answer" or "way out" will magically appear. In this way, it can be used for self or others, particularly where the emotions are involved.

The distance healing symbol, *Hon sha ze sho nen,* in addition to physical healing work, can be used as a meditation and/or prayer to heal emotional difficulties of loved ones by allowing them to access past and future power/knowledge to bring to bear upon a given situation. It can, hence, be also used to heal or alter one's karma. It is especially useful to bring healing to world situations. By concentrating on the symbol or chanting the words as a mantra, universal healing energy can be showered upon the distant situation or world leader involved through intent. It is also a marvelous technique for drumming circles to use while praying for Earth healing, and for groups or individuals.

The mental/emotional symbol can also be used to heal addictions. Reiki is said to work at the cellular and genetic levels.

Each energy medicine modality has its strengths over others. I've found that shamanism is good for some applications, Reiki is better for others and vice versa.

Reiki has a great ability to focus on physical healing. It's great for healing animals, too. After my wife Annette Waya received her Reiki attunements, on her daily walks to the post office animals from all over town would rush to meet her, just to feel the healing energy. We have treated dogs, cats... you name it.

We have horses near us now, and they love it; cats can't seem to get enough of Reiki.

Reiki is also a means for self-actualization, self-healing, and connecting with the Divine.

Various Reiki Masters have come to believe that the healing power of Reiki should be shared with minimal cost, usually only to defer the cost of training or fair compensation — a position I have adopted in my own practice. In fact, I believe everyone should be given a Reiki I attunement, as their birthright. As Reiki Master Diane Stein has said, in this time of change for people and the planet, healing is too desperately needed for it to be kept secret or exclusive any longer. [23]

While there are a myriad of books written about Reiki, I recommend these books to all my students:

Reiki: The Healing Touch: First and Second Degree Manual by William Lee Rand (Southfield, MI: Vision Publications, 1991).

The Everything Reiki Book: Channel Your Positive Energy to Reduce Stress, Promote Healing, and Enhance Your Quality of Life by Phylameana lila Desy (Cincinnati, OH: Adams Media Corporation, 2004).

Reiki and the Healing Buddha by Maureen J. Kelly (Twin Lakes, WI: Lotus Press, 2000).

The Original Reiki Handbook of Dr. Mikao Usui by Dr. Mikao Usui and Frank Arjava Petter (Twin Lakes, WI: Lotus Press, 1999).

The Book On Karuna Reiki® by Laurelle Shanti Gaia (Harsel, CO: Infinite Light Healing Studies Center Inc., 2001).

The Spirit of Reiki by Walter Lubeck, Frank Arjava Petter and William Lee Rand (Twin Lakes, WI: Lotus Press, 2002).

The great wonder of Reiki when combined with shamanism is that one does not have to 'go to the mountain' to reach its full benefits of visioning, healing and self-discovery; through the magic of the shamanic journey, the mountain comes to you! The experience of the glimpse or *kensho* of *satori* (deep, or lasting enlightenment) that Dr. Usui discovered on the fast is given to anyone who learns how to journey and accepts the attunements. It is a beautiful gift for all humankind.

Exercise 2 Learning to Be: Finding the Stillpoint

The first step in learning to listen is to develop the capability of suspending disbelief, allowing whatever chooses to show itself in the moment to come fully into consciousness, and accepting it as so. You become the Medicine Wheel, the straight lines from the center, your soul, connecting with the Powers, that radiate out to the circle of all that you perceive and encompass your world. This is a place, a space, of power. The Power is you. It is your infinite energy body extending out into time and space. It is here that you will find the Stillpoint, the quiet place of power.

You must first quiet the internal dialogue within. Extensively discussed in previous books, a few techniques can help "clear" the mind so that we can hear — truly hear — inside ourselves. This is called finding the Stillpoint. The Stillpoint is the place where one listens, all internal dialogue is silent, allowing your full presence to come forward. Throughout the ages, various spiritual paths have identified the Stillpoint in various ways, but the way always comes back to silence, stillness, being able to hear the still small voice inside that is Creator speaking.

The simplest way to find the Stillpoint is to clasp your hands in the prayer position and focus your eyes upon the middle fingers; when a thought appears in your consciousness, simply brush it aside, until internal dialogue is no more.[24]

From The Energy Notebook: Learning to See Through The Vision Quest

With the vision quest, pipe fast, or fast or extended meditation, one can learn to "see," as did Dr. Usui. It is a way of discovering or rediscovering ourselves, our "authentic selves," our "true face."

In Native America, various tribes practiced this with various modifications. Some provided vision quests for both males and females; some had vision quests for males and a separate rite of passage for girls becoming women.

In most indigenous societies, when a young boy reached puberty, he was urged to go on a vision quest under the guidance of an elder male member of the tribe. This was to give him coping tools and spiritual connection as an adult. It was a rite of passage.

In some Cherokee traditions, whole clans sometimes fasted for up to seven days, to facilitate clear thinking before a time of important decision making. Also, individuals practiced *ust'te'lisk*, going out into the woods and making a circle with 13 river stones and building a fire in its center. The person would sit with the fire, and 'feed' it all his or her questions, fears, worries and uncertainties, listening to Creator answer through the sacred fire

By all accounts, as practiced by the Native American peoples, the vision quest was at once terrifying, mystifying and life-transforming. It would begin with months of preparation and lessons taught by an elder, in ways to "see" the world. When the time was right, the boy would be taken to a remote place, far from the hustle and bustle of civilization, and left with few if any belongings. He might be left in a pit or on a mountaintop.

This elder — who could be a *wichasha waken* (Lakota) or holy man or *Didanawiskawi* (Cherokee) medicine person —

would sing and pray a discreet and respectful distance away. Afterwards, often the young man was taken to a sweat lodge (Lakota: *Inipi;* Cherokee: *Asi),* where he would recount what he saw and other elders might help him interpret his vision.

After the vision quest, the boy would be a man, with new duties, new responsibilities, a new vision and possibly a new name, given as a result of the vision.

The practice varies even among the Lakota. Peter V. Catches, for example, 38th generation Lakota medicine man of the Spotted Eagle clan, takes properly prepared individuals to quest for one day the first year, then two days the second year, then three days the third year, then four days the fourth year.[25] We have taken people for one- and two-day *us'ste'lisk,* and it has not been limited to males.

No one can adequately explain a vision from a vision quest because they are unexplainable. How can one say, for example, "a bird came... no, it was like a bird... it was an eagle... no, it was ALL eagles... and spoke to me... but it didn't say a word."

That's how my own "name" came to me years ago (the one before "PathFinder" that I use now and was given to me by a Keetowah holy man) and how it appeared to me. An eagle came flying from above. He was calling to me, wanting to speak. But I kept saying: "There aren't any eagles around here."

By his presence, he told me otherwise, but I refused to accept what I saw and heard.

So, the eagle came and landed before me and became a buzzard. Immediately, I became more at ease, for I had seen many buzzards in the area.

We carried on a conversation for a long time, each speaking wordlessly. Later, after I had dozed off or slept, or lost consciousness with my eyes open, the buzzard was an eagle again; but he was all eagles. He was also the Thunderbird.

I realized that I was seeing this great Power in the form of a bird as various cultures had seen that power. The brightness and color and intensity was from the quickly changing appearance, shifting, shimmering and flickering from each form that all beings at one time or another had perceived this power to be.

I knew the being was "really" the Thunderbird.

I knew it was also an eagle and all eagles and every winged thing and more — and that thereafter I would have the gift of speech with them, the winged things, to communicate without speaking, and they would tell me things.

He told me his name, his real name.

He told me my name.

When I passed into the next life, he wordlessly told me, my name would change to reflect that place and my being in it, as I am there, but the essential name would be the same, just a different reflection of my being in that place, from inside to outside, from outside to inside, like water reflects the sky.

There was much, much more. But, of course, none of this was said in words. Was it "real?" It was real to me. More real than "real."

A vision is a vision. It can be understood and "seen" with the heart, imagined with the brain, but understanding it with the mind is impossible.

After that, there were other visions at other times, which the vision quest introduced me to as a way of seeing the world. And, looking back, all the things I saw were things that I would see, long before I learned how to journey shamanically to see them.

For example, there was an Eagle dancer, a man dancing dressed in eagle feathers, and I now know that man is with me, my spirit guide, wherever I go.

I saw my power animal, a bear, my protector, with me always. When I do a shamanic journey, my bear takes me where I need to go and shows me what I need to see — sometimes with the eagle.

This is the power of these ancient technologies employed as Dr. Usui did in perceiving The Sacred Hoop Of Life: we are multi-dimensional beings. All the time. Our tiny awareness is like a pea in a bushel basket, rattling from one distraction to another, bouncing around the great enormity of the individual soul. It is bounded by the physical body when it comes to perception. But, we can have glimpses of the other areas where consciousness resides: in every "thing."

In the vision quest and in other sacred moments we can perceive that we are One. We can see the oneness through dreaming and shamanic journeying, in the sweat lodge, while honoring the sacred pipe through ceremony.

Moments of clarity are fleeting — often in times we set aside to Be Here Now.

From the Energy Notebook: How I "Found" Reiki

Miraculous healings have been reported by using Reiki. And I'm one of those who can attest to it: literally, a walking example of the healing power of Reiki.

I learned about Reiki while attending a shamanism workshop. In 1992, I had an accident and broke my left leg in six places from the knee down. It was shattered. The doctors didn't know if they could save it, giving me a 50-50 chance of amputation. But, after several hours of surgery, they pieced it back together, installing an 8-inch steel plate and 19 pins to hold it together.

Even so, they didn't think I would ever be able to walk normally. They said that eventually, when the technology was better developed, I would require an artificial joint for my ankle, and I spent months in a wheelchair, then more months in physical therapy learning how to walk again.

For years, the chronic pain was unbearable. It wasn't a question of *if* it hurt, but how much. Then, I went to a shamanic workshop. I whispered to my friend that my leg was hurting and a woman sitting behind us overheard and said, "I'm a Reiki master. If you would like, during the break, I'll work on your leg." I thought, well, what have I got to lose? So, I whispered back, "sure."

During the break, we went into a small side room and sat on the floor with my legs outstretched, my back against the wall. The woman held her open hands over my lower leg. My mind drifted. Suddenly, after a few moments, I noticed, my leg didn't hurt. I was dumbfounded. I said, "Lady, I don't know what you just did, but I've got to learn how to do that!"

I had never heard of Reiki. As she explained it, the vibrational level of the stainless steel in my leg was not the same as the surrounding bone and tissue and needed to be equalized. It worked. And that set me on the path to becoming a Reiki Master/Teacher myself, so that I could share this with others. That was many years ago, and I've been doing it every since: walking, even running, normally, with no pain in my leg. The scars are there, and sometimes it's a little stiff, but I walk just fine, sometimes hiking for miles. I'm literally, a walking example of the healing power of Reiki.

Since then, I've given hundreds of Reiki treatments and attunements, often with equally miraculous results — especially when combined with the shamanic journey.

Review

Reiki as shamanism:

- Recognize that steps toward self discovery and higher power are universal, and that shamanic techniques are shared among cultures and healing modalities.

- Recognize that healing power is within you and can be actualized by a simple Reiki attunement to a new level, very simply, without years of training.

- Recognize that Reiki symbols can be used to heal and to transform energy, and all is energy, for past, present and future.

- Accept that Reiki is real and part of what is shamanically "really real," or the "non-ordinary reality" of all-time, no-time.

Internet key words: *Reiki, Ki, Usui, Takata, Qigong, Shinto, Bon Po, pipe fast, vision quest.*

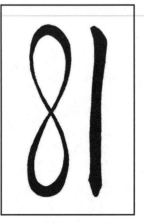

Pathfinder Reiki Symbol

Active Threshold

Beginning

Chapter Three

Healing Through
The Shamanic Journey

Rather than being a seeker, be a finder.

— ASCENSION TESTS

People speak a great deal about "ancient knowledge" that can be used to guide us, frequently referring to the Egyptians, Greeks, and the Aztec and Mayan cultures of the Americas. Christ was born about 2,000 years ago, perhaps 4 AD; the classical period of Greece started around 480 BC; Buddha, Siddhartha Gautama, was born around 563 BC, the Great Pyramid in Egypt was built around 2550 BC; the Mayan calendar begins around 3114 BC; the oldest parts of the Bible refer to the times of Enoch and the prophet Elijah, during the time of the Sumerians, around 3500 BC. So, the oldest of these sources are about 5,000–6,000 years old.

The most ancient of the spiritual technologies available to us, however, is shamanism. It is believed to be 30,000–45,000 years old.[1] To give an idea of how long ago that was, the short, stocky, hairy Neanderthals were supplanted in Europe some 30,000 years ago. It can reliably be said that shamanism is the most ancient healing technology of all that is still extant and practiced, virtually unaltered among remote tribes, and by solitary practitioners worldwide.

The modern human brain and physique, given the historic pace of evolution, are also essentially the same as 30,000 years ago or more, the scientists tell us. Modern diet and health care makes bigger, taller and, in some cases, stronger humans. But we're basically the same creatures that were practicing shamanism tens of thousands of years ago.

One of the main differences is our cultural conceit. We believe that because we have greater technology and more information that we know more. In fact, humans generally know less now because they aren't required to learn the basics of survival or how to depend on their inner resources for life's many challenges. In many ways, our ancestors knew more about the real world, daily living and survival than we know now.

If the lives of indigenous peoples are seen to be primitive it is because our technological advancement has made food, housing, travel and communication seemingly effortless, plentiful, and easily available. Obscured by modern conveniences and deluded by media shortcuts to understanding the world around us (ie, television images and "sound bytes" to inform us, rather than first-person observation and detailed conversations with others), our knowledge of the "real" world as a spiritual place (what's "really real," or that which underlies physical reality) and the beings who inhabit it is simplified, fictionalized and made false. That which is real is made to appear unreal and that which is unreal is made to appear normal. There is a great deal of difference between purchasing food at a well-stocked grocery store — or via the Internet! — and actually searching for, stalking and capturing, killing or gathering one's food. This is not a condemnation of modern human beings. Technology is a boon, but we forget sometimes that it is a double-edged sword, and both sides always play out eventually. The point is, what is lost? Which world is the "real" world? How we approach our world, with mindfulness, and gratitude, and appreciation is essential to truly seeing and being in each moment.

In sum: the humans using the tools of shamanism thousands of years ago are basically the same as humans living today. The wiring of the brain is the same; the physical body is the same. What is "really real" hasn't changed. Only our Dream Of The World (the image we hold in our minds and attach to outside of us that causes us believe and act as we do in this plane of existence) has changed, and it seems to be coming full circle, so to speak, regarding science and spirituality. Our greatest minds today tell us that the "real" world is not so real. For example, Gary Zukov says, as far as light (patterns of energy) and matter (patterns of energy) are concerned, there is no distinction between "what is" and "what happens." The dance and the dancer are one.[2] Observation, our thoughts, our emotions, and our intellect can change matter and energy. This is what physicists call QUIP, the Quantum Inseparability Principle, that every particle affects every other particle, everywhere, and that everything is the cause of everything, every which way in time.[3] The universe has been described as pure movement, vibration loaded with the potential to manifest into an infinite array of patterns; "probability in motion." In total, it is a vibrating system of conscious energy, from which all things are composed — a proto-intelligence found in realities of greater and greater subtlety, each plane or dimension orders of magnitude removed from the next.[4] It is even posited that this explains how knowledge discovered in one place is discovered simultaneously elsewhere.[5]

So, even our cutting edge scientists tell us that the world is much greater, more diverse, more responsive, synergistic and alive than we are led to believe — astoundingly, as our ancient forebears and shamans, mystics and seers have said for thousands of years. In our popular culture, TV series such as *Ghost Whisperer* and *Medium,* promote the idea that "the occult" is scary or unique to certain people, when in fact, through the shamanic techniques of using the drum, or even nighttime dreaming, we are capable of accessing, seeing, being in and affecting the real world. Those who write about shamanic experiences call shamanic seeing as being in nonordinary reality. In this instance, though, by labeling the shamanic experience as "nonordinary" reality, we are to an extent falsely describing it, for nonordinary reality is actually our reality, accessed by using all of our senses, not merely the five bodily sense organs. By failing to acknowledge the use of spiritual tools that have been available for thousands of years we may be robbing ourselves of the greatest gift our ancestors bequeathed to us: the ability to readily access the divine in our lives, around us and within us.

The modern human being is perfectly suited to practicing shamanism. The practices are attuned to the body/mind — the same as they have been for thousands of years — and can open up whole new worlds of inner and outer vision. No matter where our minds — science, or Dream of The World — may lead us, we are still a part of the whole, linked with nature. Basic to the human condition, the natural condition of humankind is the spiritual connection. If we lose sight of the spiritual, we have lost sight of ourselves, who we are and our soul purpose.

I believe all humans are born as Children of Earth and Sky; our mother, the Earth, from which our bodies are formed, and the Sky, Creator, light and Great Mind, Great Being, Great Spirit. Without this connection between Creator and Earth, with all the Powers of the Earth and Sky, we as human beings are vulnerable to feeling dissociated from the world, empty and without purpose.

The benefits of seeing beyond the material world and actually affecting healing in ourselves and for those around us through practicing such ancient spiritual technologies as Reiki and shamanism is life changing for those who endeavor to try it.

Shamanic healing doesn't need drugs

The healing aspect of shamanism, and as a guide for personal spiritual development, uses a natural, non-drug induced, altered state of consciousness brought on by rhythmic percussion and ritual to facilitate health in self and others. One does not need drugs of any kind to achieve the shamanic state, it's natural, as natural as dreaming at night or day dreaming. All the "chemicals" one needs are already in our bodies, as Candace Pert, the neuroscientist who discovered the opiate receptor, the cellular bonding site for endorphins in the brain, and others have proven. Indeed, outside chemicals only interfere, either by blocking access to the sensitivity needed to "see." Or, in the case of strong psychotropic drugs, 'blowing off the doors' of the ability to discern reality from nonreality. People come to me who have had experiences with shamans in Central and South America who use psychotropic drugs in their traditional rituals, and have lost the ability of discernment. It is usually either the result of someone who took part in one of these rituals without proper guidance, or lacked the proper training to keep balance. There should be great caution here. In recent years, taking ayahuasca (Quechua, pronounced aye-yah-waska), a psychoactive brew prepared from the *Banisteriopsis* vine native to the Amazon, has become quite popular among some groups, particularly young people, who believe they can be magically transformed into becoming "shamans" by taking the drug.

As a shamanic practitioner of nearly 40 years, I can attest that it is inappropriate and dangerous because not only is the informing/balancing/grounding context of the ritual missing — which is a way of life — but also the plant is not native; therefore, people outside the area where it grows may have no affinity for it or relationship with it. It is a Western way of thinking, like taking a vitamin C pill rather than eating an orange, that shamanism can be learned by simply taking a drug. Even with vitamins, we now understand that their context, the food, is important to the way the vitamin works, and that isolating the "active ingredient" is misguided. For example, as with ayahuasca and its proper and carefully controlled use among South American shamans, in the Native American Church, where peyote is taken as a sacrament, the context within which the drug is taken very nearly negates it as a drug per se. It becomes instead an enhancement of the spiritual vitality and force of the ceremonial prayer in the context of honoring the Earth and all beings. Peyote in this context is a spiritual being who joins in the ceremony and allows a deeper experience of song and prayer. Without the church ceremony, the songs, the leaders and the communal gathering, or the sacred context, if you will, taking peyote would be simply abusing a drug.

Discernment is the first rule of shamanism, being able to discern who, what and how things are around you, and how you fit within the energetic scheme, knowing exactly where your energy — seen and unseen — is going. It's a constant test. Discernment can be seen as a very definition of shamanism, one who can see in non-ordinary reality but cannot cope in what is considered ordinary reality is not a shaman but a lunatic. One must be able to "walk between the worlds" with ease, able to ground fully and use five-sense perceptions in the 3-D world and step into nonordinary reality and back again in order to truly master the craft of shamanism. Use of drugs to obtain the shamanic state can destroy this ability of keeping discernment and maintaining harmony and balance that mark the shaman, though it may be regained, with great effort. Many young people have come to me after taking drugs thinking it would enhance their perception, turn them into shamans, but they have had to learn the rudiments of grounding, centering and shielding from the beginning, starting all over again just to regain normal functioning. It's a long and arduous process to rebuild the foundations of perception that can be shattered so easily by ill-advised use of drugs. Using drugs to attain a "shamanic" state can also become a crutch that limits shamanic ability — the freedom to choose that comes from discernment, unfettered by attachments to the material world, in this case, physical or psychological addiction to a drug. It can prevent those just starting out from developing their own personal power and limit their ability to explore various avenues of perception that are available only by being fully aware and unclouded by physical and psychological effects. Through use of the drum or in nightly dreaming, shamanic ability is naturally obtained and sustainable without the use of any outside drug.

The dis-eases of modern life that shamanic practices have been demonstrated to help with include: depression, feeling fragmented, dealing with loss, chronic pain or illness, personal empowerment, childhood/past traumas, recovering from accidents.

Shamanism can also be used for: distance healing, healing the Earth, blessing homes, crops and businesses, accessing the spirits of a place, helping souls enter the afterlife (Psychopomp), divination, finding life purpose, recovering lost objects, recovering lost or stolen soul pieces, spirit depossession

A practitioner, or "healer" (I use in quotation marks, because the person who comes for help heals him or herself; the other is a facilitator) who has had adequate training can perform these tasks with varying degrees of success. Even in tribal cultures, individuals who do this work possess greater abilities in one area over another.

The skeptical must ask, does shamanism really heal?

First one must consider the nature of "dis-ease." In the shamanistic way of viewing the world, disease can come about through:

1. Loss of a person's guardian spirit (loss of "luck," protection from unfortunate events, illness).

2. Suffering a spiritual intrusion (energy is drained, diverted or blocked; depression, anger or a physical ailment can be the result of a spiritual intrusion).

3. Soul loss: loss of life force energy (feeling apart from life, depression/suicidal, addiction; post-traumatic syndrome; excessive grief/mourning).[6]

Shamanic techniques do not supplant Western medical help, but can act as a less intrusive way to help the individual heal his/her own wounds or aid in modern medical practice. It is called a form of complementary or alternative medicine (CAM) for this reason, and is recognized by the National Institute of Health as conducive to health and wellness.[7] Such complementary modalities strike at the heart of "healing," as opposed to "curing." Healing is bringing back into spiritual harmony/balance. But unless someone changes the relationships that caused the dis-ease, the person will not be "cured."

We often hold on to the situations that cause loss of personal power (dis-ease) because they are our patterns of life. Though painful, they are our "cross to bear" in life. At least, that's what we perceive our lives to be either through family expectations, education, background, cultural beliefs, or other factors (our Dream of The World).

A healer can perform the rituals that work to restore human health and vitality, as tribal cultures have done for 30,000 years or more, but it's up to the individual to maintain health or accept the life force energy that's given back, in a meaningful way.

An example: consider a child who is an incest survivor. A piece of that child's soul may be shed to block out the pain. Over the years, the individual feels that loss, though doesn't know why, and it's reflected in day-to-day living as a loss of vitality, a sense of meaninglessness in life or through non-productive behaviors. The shamanic healer would see this as requiring soul retrieval. The healer can often retrieve that soul piece, bring back the dreamer, the lost innocence, the joy that was lost through that traumatic event. But, it is up to the adult to accept the soul piece lost during childhood and allow room in his/her life for it to find expression so it won't be lost again. (By the way, soul loss can occur at any time, at any age, through any event or trauma — from auto accidents, divorce, business failures, as well as early childhood or adolescent events.)

Circumventing the Rational Mind

The essential technology of shamanic healing is the drum, which allows the practitioner to enter non-ordinary reality and effect healing. It does so by circumventing the rational mind. Even how the drum accomplishes that fact remains a mystery. It's certain that the rhythmic beating of the drum — about 70 beats per minute — can induce a trance state. That's the rational mind speaking. But matters of the heart lack force and power when filtered through the rational mind and things aren't always what they seem. Often, what seems true is only partially true. We do know that the ability to see nonordinary reality has been around for thousands of years and somehow that ability has been discounted or all but lost. "Inducing a trance state" doesn't come close to explaining the power of the drum or the ability to enter nonordinary reality. Ancient humans knew there were many ways to access the divine, or at least get a glimpse that transcended the repetitive chatter of the rational mind (the left brain, or rational portion), the "little mind," to perceive that which is greater, or the Great Mind of God.

Today, we know that chakras or energy centers in the body do exist because they can be scientifically measured. Three thousand years ago, in Eastern cultures, it was a reality because those who could ascertain the vortices of energy emanating from the human body could perceive them by techniques that circumvented the chattering mind. Those techniques, or ancient technologies, are available to us today. And many of them are still being practiced on the American continent by people who have retained this knowledge for thousands of years, despite centuries of persecution.

Shamans still practice and are important parts of their communities in South and Central America, often in remote regions. The closest we can come to shamanism in its purest form in North America is through the philosophy of traditional Native Americans in general and the practices of medicine men and women in particular. It is a powerful teaching and way of looking at the world equal to any of the ancient cultures in China, Egypt, India, Tibet or other parts of the world.[8] In fact, the indigenous people of the pre-Columbian Americas were among the few peoples of the Earth who had a civilization that ancient Buddhists in Tibet considered enlightened. In *The Tibetan Book of the Dead,* devout Buddhists were taught more than 1,000 years ago how to choose a body for reincarnation.[9] These choices were divined by seers adept at spiritual body travel and only a very few places were listed as suitable for reincarnation. Although most of the world according to these seers was not recommended for soul recycling, a few geographical locations were listed as areas where souls could find peace, long life and comfortable prosperity, including China, Egypt, Asia, the Mideast and the Indian subcontinent.

These seers also described the Americas, which they named "Kuru," as having "lakes" of "cattle," that were, no doubt, buffalo dotting the Great Plains, and "evergreens," probably referring to the land of the Eastern Woodland Indians, possibly the land of the Iroquois and Cherokee. Europe 1,000 years ago was not recommended. There was a reason for the suitability of being reborn in the Americas in the thinking of these seers, as distinguished from European societies. Native Americans were adept at right-brain thinking, as were pre-and early Christian societies in the Mid east — the type of consciousness that accommodates shamanism. They were able to tap into what Carl Jung called the collective unconscious, the archetypes of dreams and actually perceive (if not enter) that non-ordinary reality. Shamanic journeying, using the drum, is nothing more than dreaming, except it is directed by the mind and more easily retained than in the nighttime dream state. It is available to everyone and as natural as sleeping — or, perhaps more accurately, maintaining that state between full waking and slipping into sleep. Perhaps "heavy day dreaming" is a more accurate term!

Those who know nothing about it sometimes claim that shamanism is anti-religious, sacrilegious or "pagan." Hardly. Most Christian churches in America today circulate prayer lists or form prayer circles for those in need. Shamanic healing could accurately be called "visualized prayer." And the definition of a pagan is anyone who is not a Christian, Muslim or Jew. Americans of all faiths can and do practice shamanism, usually resulting in a deeper, firmer and richer appreciation of faith. How can it be sacrilegious for a Christian, Muslim or Jew to see and speak with angels and aid souls on their way to the Afterlife?

Both pre-Christians (the Essenes most notably) and early Christians (Gnostics and others) incorporated shamanic practices — although they didn't call them that. The word shaman is of Siberian origin, meaning "one who sees in the dark." Many shamans, in fact, don't like being called a shaman for that implies that the power to help others belongs to them. The power belongs to the Creator and the work is done by their power animals and guides. They are merely the facilitators. Being a shaman or practicing shamanism is a moment-by-moment experience, not a quality of being, and hence it cannot be awarded a certificate or title.

People in biblical times were well versed in perceiving and appreciating non-ordinary reality. Angels are commonplace in both the Bible and the Qur'an (where they are termed *mala'ikah* — literally "one with power"). Muhammed was inspired to write the Qur'an by the angel Gabriel and the sacred book relates that people at all times have two angels observing them, called the *Kiraman Katibeen*, or Noble Writers, that record our every deed. (Angels are recognized in traditional Native American societies, as well. In Cherokee, we refer to angels as *adawi*, and/or beings of above, *galvlati*).

The angels haven't disappeared. We just don't use our right brains to see them, or to recognize non-ordinary reality as people did in biblical times. For example, in the excluded Gnostic book of the *Infancy Gospel of James*, in which angels appeared to both Mary and Joseph, Joseph relates what could be called a perception of non-ordinary reality after he placed Mary in the cave to give birth to Jesus.[10]

Joseph went to find a midwife. But as he was walking, he noticed that everyone else was standing still. Birds were suspended in mid-air, sheep that were being driven were motionless, with the shepherd's hand frozen, upraised to strike. This is the type of vision that can be tapped into when journeying shamanically, when time and space are suspended, except by the observer, who is carried along by the intent of consciousness. It can be seen as a moment in time in which a portal opened. This is due to the significance of the birth for humankind, and because this particular moment in time has been a focus for generation upon generation of humans since the event, causing it to be affected by the intent of mass humanity. It can be seen as an unfocused example of the power of prayer in all-time, no time. Real reality, or what is called nonordinary reality, and the "place" where healing is done, is a circle, a circle in time. It has no beginning and no end. When one achieves this state in the shamanic journey, the practitioner is at a place where healing can occur, here, there, anywhere.

An example of how pre-and early Christian society perceived the effects of using non-ordinary reality to heal is the story of a 'possessed' child shortly after Jesus was born. It is in *The First Gospel of the Infancy of Jesus Christ,* an excluded Gnostic text of the second century AD, first translated into English in 1697. It's said that Mary had washed Jesus' swaddling clothes and hung them out to dry upon a post. The priest's son, said to have been possessed by the devil, put the cloths on his head and immediately, "the devils began to come out of his mouth, and fly away in the shape of crows and serpents."[11]

In the language of the time the text was written, the boy's dis-ease was seen as being possessed by demons. Actually, in shamanic terms, he was afflicted by what's called a "spiritual intrusion." Modern-day shamanic practitioners are adept at removing these energy forms, which can be described as low-level patterns of energy that cause disruption in the normal functioning of the aural body. It is a technique that requires only a little training but does require some skill. (The key is to remove only what needs removing and allow what needs to be there to stay there.) It is taught under other names, such as psychic surgery, in some other vibrational medicine modalities.[12]

The description of the emanation from the boy's mouth, crows and serpents, are Jungian universal archetypes. Crows are generally considered messengers; snakes (when not showing fangs) are considered symbols of re-birth, renewal and wisdom. It's written that Essene initiates to higher learning were given the snake as a symbol for their new life.

The story is related in the early Christian text not because the healing was unusual — the Essenes were renowned for such shamanic healings, the word Essene was often used interchangeably with "healer" — but because it was the infant Christ's clothes that healed, showing His miraculous power.

In Joseph's case, although the reason for the suspension of time was the awesome event of Christ's birth, the fact that it was relayed in Scripture shows the people of the time understood the concept of the laws of time and space being suspended during momentous events. People today usually only experience such perceptions when faced with a crisis, such as a near-death experience or in an auto accident or other event where latent powers are activated.[13]

Perhaps the most powerful example of a non-ordinary reality event is included in the excluded Gnostic texts regarding Christ's death. After He was crucified, several who were acquainted with Him reported that He appeared to them in different places simultaneously. To some, He appeared normally; to others He shifted from child to man to child and other forms, flickering in his appearance. This describes an effect of shamanic journeying called projection or shapeshifting. The followers of Christ saw His spirit body as projected to them. Nor is it limited in chronological time. The appearance of "The Pale One," told in Cherokee lore, in legends around the world, are legion, both before Christ's birth and after His death. Whether the Pale One was Christ, or an appearance of Christ Consciousness — in the Americas called Quetzalcoatl — is a matter of interpretation, and considerable speculation.[14]

As noted earlier, in sacred geometry (which both the Essenes and Egyptians believed in), a person's energy body describes a star tetrahedron, with twin vortices of energy spinning in opposite directions. This energy body extends 27 feet in each direction in this dimension, but also extends into other dimensions. Energetically speaking, shamanic journeying can be said to follow the lines of the practitioner's merkaba into other dimensions.

The very term merkaba is ancient Hebrew. The letters that spell out the word Mer-ka-ba are *Mem-Raish-Caf-Bet*, from the original root word, *Raish-Caf-Bet,* meaning to ride, but usually is translated as chariot, sometimes as wagon. At one time, such journeying into time and space was part of the teaching of the Kabbala, the mystical tradition of Judaism, as the merkaba meditation. It is believed that Elijah, who may have been a member of a Jewish mystery school, used the merkaba to transcend space and time in the whirlwind or chariot of fire recounted in II Kings. Presumably, Jesus as a youth would be acquainted with this mystical teaching, as it was prevalent in the Mideast at the time.

His simultaneous appearance can be described in terms of harmonics and entrainment. To borrow from the analogy of nine-year-old Joey, an example would be a long-distance trucker traveling down the highway talking on a citizens band radio that has been illegally boosted far beyond the legal 4-watt limit, with people living a mile or so away picking up his "Breaker-Breaker, Good Buddy... " on their stereos and TVs. The original signal is so powerful it can be picked up by receivers tuned to other frequencies through the principle of harmonics — or waves that are fractions of the original wave or frequency.

In the excluded *Gnostic Secret Gospel of John,* Christ appears as a flickering shape, from a child, to an elderly person, to a servant, to several forms until He stabilized into His human visage as "one figure with several forms within the light."[15] This was a manifestation of Christ seeking to find entrainment with the viewer. The variability of the vision — from child to ancient to servant — was the intent of Christ seeking to find resonance within the perception of John. Once resonance was found, entrainment (or stabilization of the image) could occur.

A Native American medicine man or woman — or witness to their routine work — would recognize immediately the significance of the "miracles" described in the ancient Gnostic texts. With the priest's son, the "crows" are symbolic, but the vision is real. The healing is real. Such an event is only "miraculous" to one who hasn't seen it.

It is important to note when doing shamanic work that all that is seen, or perceived, is in symbolic, visionary form. The beings and truths are perceived in the way in which the viewer is able to perceive them. So, every time we journey, or dream for that matter, we must bear in mind that the images that are presented to us are in symbolic form, with more than face value meaning, often many layers of meaning. We perceive and are perceived in varying ways in Dreamtime. For example, suppose you dream or see in a shamanic journey, a bear trap squarely in your path. When you awaken, or write down what you saw, you must not only recognize that you saw a bear trap, but note also what a bear trap means to you. It probably does not mean that you will step in a bear trap, unless you happen to live in a locale where bears are trapped; rather, that you may face a trap or potential problem, a sticking point, that only the quality of "bear" can determine, involve or solve. So, in this, the rational mind can be carefully employed to discern the meaning of the symbology of Dreamtime or the shamanic journey.

As we have seen, the chakra system is a pattern of energy, which is itself, composed of the patterns of the separate chakras themselves. Each human being has his or her own patterns that can be brought into cohesion and projected wherever the dreamer wants to go through nightly dreaming or through shamanic journeying techniques.

In either case, it is then the intent of the dreamer that determines the destination or the purpose of the journey. We are multi-dimensional beings — all the time. At any time, and all the time, our body/mind frequencies are going out and coming back to us. That is the power we each have as oscillators through the human heart, pushing electrical waves through our body systems, or merkabas. We must only quiet the mind or distract it in order to "see" and direct our interactions in other dimensions or levels of reality. We quiet or redirect our attention in order to perceive the Dreamtime that we access all the time, not only in night time dreaming.

In shamanic journeying, we can let our consciousness "ride the wave" of those frequencies and come back with new knowledge, new insights, visions and intelligences that we can use for healing others and ourselves.

Learning to journey shamanically

So, how does one learn how to journey? In Native American and other indigenous societies, shamans or medicine men and women were selected either by the tribe members who carefully observed children for shamanic abilities, or by individuals themselves who had visionary experiences that pre-ordained them to become healers.

Third gender children (that today we call "gay") were frequently selected as healers and sages. Early French trappers gave these esteemed healers, often men dressed as women, the name *berdache*. They were often called "two-Spirits."

Often, visionary abilities would occur during illness and near-death experiences. Black Elk said he had his first visionary experience at the age of nine, while ill, but didn't know what to do with it. It wasn't until he undertook his vision quest at 18 that the earlier vision was explained to him and then it only had value, he said, because he acted out his vision.[16]

There's a valuable instruction there. Just as Native American peoples have long believed that dreams were messages from the Creator, they believed they must be shared with others and brought into reality, even if only in symbolic fashion. It is important, when Power instructs you to do something, to do it. Otherwise, you may lose the ability to discern Power or the revelation of the Great Mystery.

Most people today take a workshop to learn how to journey. For example, The Foundation for Shamanic Studies (FSS) in Mill Valley, Calif., offers workshops across the country to teach people "core shamanism," as developed by anthropologist Michael Harner.[17] The workshops begin with the basic Way of the Shaman course and progress to various advanced techniques. This "core" shamanism is derived from shamanic practices documented in various cultures that are consistent among shamans in all nations. The basic workshop teaches how to journey using the drum, how to access one's power animal, or guiding spirit, and gives a framework for understanding non-ordinary reality. Even when dedicated students come to me, I usually recommend they take a course first, so that they can learn the basics, as it takes years to truly learn shamanism. The basics are fairly universal. Non-ordinary reality is often defined as the lower world, the middle world and the upper world.

The lower world is where power animals reside. It can appear as anything, but requires going through a long tunnel or perhaps a series of caves to arrive there. It is characterized as a dark place deep within the Earth. It has been described in myth and folklore as the place where other realities can be found, such as the River Styx, where the dead "cross over," as the place where Pluto reigns and Persephone travels to while the energies of the surface are in winter and life is below, and where magical, mystical beings reside. It's going down the rabbit hole in *Through the Looking-Glass,* where everything is topsy-turvy, with its own illogical laws and improbable, though powerful denizens. Indeed, in shamanic journey, this is where power animals reside and a shaman is sometimes asked to go to retrieve a power animal. What is not commonly taught is that the lower world is where one can travel through time; visiting the Earth or other worlds at any time in past or future. It's not the "dark" place some would imagine, but hosts any number of realities. For example, on my very first journey, I was taken to the underworld on the back of an eagle and shown a world of evergreens. We landed in a glade and I walked to a small hill where I saw an older, wizened man sitting before a fire. I marveled at how calm he appeared, and wise, and thought: "Gosh, I wish I could be like that." And my power animal, the eagle, laughed and said: "You will be! That is you, some nine years from now." And indeed, it came true. I became that man, and sitting in front of that fire, in those evergreens, remembered the flight on the back of an eagle those many years before.

The middle world is the "real" world, where we live, but seen through the eyes of non-ordinary reality. This is useful in 'scoping out distance places, doing long-distance healing and other aspects; it's great for finding lost glasses or car keys. You can journey to see the plants and animals who share our world, listen to what they have to tell us and perhaps learn their songs and their secrets, so that we can help and heal them and others.[18]

The upper world is where the spirit guides and teachers reside, as well as other dimensions. Most of my work is in the upper world. In the first level of the upper world, as it appears to me, is whatever my spirit animal chooses for me to see. This is an area where I do a lot of healing work, particularly working on people's auras, chakra balancing, and soul work. I call it The Sky Lodge. It's difficult to describe but this is where I do my long-distance work, where I'm both in the upper world doing the work and also wherever the person actually is located. I have clients all across the country and some in foreign countries. Space and time are suspended in non-ordinary reality, so the client can be anywhere. In this place, I look down at the person who is to be treated and see the person's energetic form. I do not see any physical surroundings or the physical structure of the person (short, tall, fat, thin, dark, light, etc.).

In the second level is "the void," which is an absence of anything and pitch black, surrounded by a star-filled universe. I find a lot of lost or shed soul pieces in this area. At the edge of that place, near the void, in the star universe, resides my totem, which is a bird of many colors and shapes, which some call a Thunderbird.

In the third level, one passes through the star-void universe and hits a multi-colored grid. I've done a lot of healing work for people as groups at the grid and for karmic matters and for my Higher Power to interact with others' Higher Powers. Passing through that, which is called by some the Christ Consciousness Grid or Plume of Quetzalcoatl or the Akashic Field, one can find the place where the highest guides reside.

As you practice journeying, ask your power animal to take you to these places, and become familiar with them. But don't be surprised if your "map" of nonordinary reality differs, perhaps considerably. I am constantly learning new areas and finding that my concepts — lower world, middle world, upper world — may not coincide with what is found or fit within my framework of thought. For example, how do I "enter" the lower world? I don't physically go through a hole, and the hole doesn't even have to be at hand. It could be the sink in the kitchen, the next room, or a bole in a tree outside in the yard, or a cave that I visited once. I simply "go there" in my mind's eye, and I'm "there" shamanically. The lower world can have whole worlds with skies and trees and bodies of water, including its own "upper" world. There are whole universes to discover in nonordinary reality, and no one has the only map. It is fun to compare what you see with others who also journey shamanically, and a frequent game that is played by those first learning how to journey is to play "tag." Both journey, and one tries to find the other in nonordinary reality. It can be quite revealing!

Let the Drum Take You

As frequently taught, the drumming begins and the student envisions going down into a hole, perhaps at the base of a tree, or for those who live in cities, it could even be drain or pipe. Where one comes out could be anywhere, and the student could continue in the lower world or go to the middle world or up to the upper world.[19] When going on a shamanic journey, we are guided by intent. We may wish to help someone by retrieving a power animal for them. If so, your intent is to go to the lower world. Or, you wish to check out a specific place (middle world) and go to the upper world. Or, you might want to just go into non-ordinary reality and see what your power animals, guides and angels have to tell you. Whatever your intent, the drum begins and you enter the tunnel, where you are met by your power animal, who takes you where you ask to go.

Learning to drum and journey at the same time takes considerable practice; it's easier to have someone else drum or listen to a recording. You can record yourself drumming for use at a later time, but recordings are commercially available online, as well.

There is nothing esoteric about journeying shamanically, despite what some would make it out to be; it is simply viewing the world in a different way or, more accurately, allowing ourselves to view the world in a different way. I've taught, or helped teach, hundreds of people how to journey and all have been able to journey, although some have needed more help than others.

If you are having difficulty journeying, it could be useful to practice "seeing" in nighttime dreaming, that is, going to Dreamtime, and "seeing" there. Keep a notepad by your bed, and just before going to sleep resolve to remember all dreams and write them down immediately upon waking. Over time, not only will you automatically begin recalling dreams but also you will consciously participate in them, thus gaining more insight into their meaning and increasing power over your consciousness. To do this, apply the simple yet effective technique taught to Carlos Castaneda by his teacher, Don Juan: while dreaming, remember to look for your hands, because when you find them you can control the dream.[20] As you begin to gain proficiency in "seeing" in nighttime dreaming, you will find that reaching the shamanic state will become simpler, too.

Four Ways of Using Energy

There are four basic ways a person can heal using energy medicine: channeling, reflecting, taking on, and melding.

Channeling allows a divine being, or beings, to use the body as a hollow bone for healing. This is the type of energy work used with Reiki, and with Reiki in the shamanic state.

Reflecting is using your energy field to reflect back to the person, plant or animal what is missing or out of balance with the one being treated.

Taking on is a rather difficult and potentially very dangerous method whereby the dis-ease is taken on by the healing practitioner and healed. It's generally not advised.[21]

Melding (or blending) is becoming one with the person, plant or animal being treated, so that dis-eases may be removed. This also is a tricky maneuver, not advised with human beings, since you are mingling your personal energy with another's and can "take on" dis-ease, and it's important that the other person not "take on" your patterns of energy, as well, but it can work well with plants and animals, if one is firmly grounded, centered and shielded.[22]

In all of this work, you must be careful in how you use energy. It is important that you are discerning in your use of energy, using personal energy very rarely, relying instead on the energy of the Earth or the Powers to effect ceremony or perform healing. If you become tired doing energy work, it means you are depleting your personal energy. Allow Earth energy or Reiki energy to pass through you. Even with prayer, one expends only a relatively small amount of energy, enough to provide guidance and structure, while allowing Power to come through. Creator does the work. It doesn't do any good, or make the effect any better, by praying "harder." Pray better, not harder; direct your intent toward achieving the ceremony, allowing miracles to happen. Detach from the outcome. Creator creates the miracles.

Mix Them Up

In my practice, Reiki is often used in distance healing, using shamanic journey when appropriate. Frequently, when someone is hospitalized either through particularly acute illness or accident, I will be called to assist. To do this, I have a stuffed cloth figure that I use, placing it in a medicine circle, which includes carefully selected crystals, while invoking the Reiki power symbol over Hon sha ze sho nen.

Once the person is stabilized, I may also incorporate drumming or shamanic journeying to work on the patient's aura with the Reiki guides.

Reiki and shamanic journeying work quite well together. For example, it has become my standard practice when doing long-distance soul retrieval to reform the client's aura with the Reiki guides when finishing up. After doing a soul retrieval in person, I'll remove any spiritual intrusions there may be (which is also taught under the name of psychic surgery in advanced Reiki training) and then use Reiki to reform the aura and implant Reiki healing symbols to seal it.

Experiment, practice, use Reiki in your daily life, in Dreamtime and in the shamanic journey. It is through these inner and outer journeys that we develop as healers of self and All Our Relations.

Exercise 3 Going on The Shamanic Journey

The steps for shamanic journey are very simple. Most people begin to learn how to journey by traveling to the underworld to meet their power animal. The power animal is a being — actually, a power of the universe — that accompanies you wherever you go. We are each born with one to attend to us. Remember that fuzzy bear you carried around as a child? Or the unicorn? Or tiger? That was probably your power animal — or totem — from birth. We usually refer to power animals as animals, because animals are universal upon this planet and have recognizable qualities — such as bears and tigers being fierce protectors, while also furry and cuddly — but the attending power can be anything. They change through time. Although your totem may last throughout your lifetime, power animals come and go. Usually, you have at least one, though some people — shamans particularly — can have whole menageries.

So, to begin, turn on your tape or CD of drumming, or have a friend drum a steady beat for you, approximately 70 beats per minute. Any type of drum is fine, although a single-sided hand drum is easy to hold for long periods. A good first journey is 15 minutes. It may be useful to cover your eyes with a cloth to block out the light. Lie down, take a few deep breaths, and clear your mind. Imagine yourself in a cool, dark place, a waiting place, and a good place to begin your journey. It could be a cave, or a place on a beach that you particularly enjoy. The main thing is that you want to have a hole nearby that you can go down into. Perhaps there is a tree with a bole in it in a park near your house. Or it could be a bridge that is dark underneath near your home. Some people even go down the kitchen drain!

After you have gained some proficiency at journeying, it is here where your power animal will come to greet you, at this waiting place, to take you above or below or outward into one of the three worlds. But, this time, we want to go down the hole, whatever it may be, to meet our power animal. It could very well be that your power animal will show up now, even before you have entered the hole; it could be any type of animal, but you will recognize it for its friendliness; it will exude an aura of goodness — no sharp teeth or threatening mannerisms. It will also show you at least three different aspects of itself; for example, sideways, frontward and backwards. In Native way, when an animal shows itself to you in one of its sacred poses, it is lending you its power, and showing you that you are connected. Your power animal will seek to show you that it belongs to you and you belong to it, in this way.

If your power animal shows itself to you in this waiting place, that's fine. Go with it, but if not, then imagine going down the hole you have chosen, going down, down, down, past roots of trees, through rocks (remember, you are in spirit form, you can go through anything, or around anything, or jump over anything — there is no limit to your powers, getting big or getting small, as the need arises). Keep going down, down, down, until you finally arrive somewhere. You will know you are there, because you will stop. Look around. It's likely you will see many power animals, and beings; or you may see none at all. Whatever you see, look at it for later reference. But if there are many beings, remember that your power animal will show you itself in three different poses, and its energy will be one of connection and support.

Once your power animal connects with you, allow it take you for a journey; hop on its back, or let it guide you as you fly. The sky isn't the limit; the horizons are limitless. After 15 minutes have your friend drum you back, that is, double the tempo of the drum with the intent of energetically pulling you back into this reality. Your friend should say: "OK, time to come back!" And you should wiggle your toes and stretch your fingers, allowing all your energy to come back into your physical body.

When you have come back, relate what you have seen; write it down carefully for future reference. Often, while in shamanic journey, what you see may not make a great deal of sense. But in shamanic journey, everything is symbolic. Having a vision of a wall, for example, may not be a physical wall, but a barrier that you are experiencing in your life. If there were, for example, writing on the wall that said something like "look for blue skies," it could mean that the solution to that problem in your life will be solved by a place, activity or behavior relating to blue skies. Suppose you were having difficulty at work and had been thinking about taking a trip to the beach, but it seemed there was so much to do at work that you couldn't get away. The message would be: go to the beach, the barriers preventing you from moving forward will dissolve then.

It should be noted that the area of the brain used for seeing in shamanic journey is adjacent to the area of imagination. So, the best way to learn how to see in shamanic journey, if you have difficulty, is to use your imagination at first. That is, imagine that you are going down into the lower world, imagine that you are seeing a power animal, etc. As time goes by, and you repeatedly journey, you will find that there is less "imagination" than dreaming, or journeying that is "real." It's a question of quality; simply slipping over from suggesting (imagining) visions or insights, to actually having visions and insights seemingly unbidden.

Once you have met your power animal, always remember not to leave home without it! It is a

Power of the Universe and will protect you from all harm, no matter how great the potential threat. If nothing else, it will sling you into another universe to escape harm, allowing you to return safely. This goes for Dreamtime, too. In nighttime journey, connect with your power animal; simply ask it to appear, and it will. Whether you call this way of seeing astral travel, shamanic journey, or simply dreaming, it is important that we call upon the Powers to guide and protect us, so that we may see and learn safely. It's a big universe — or universes! — out there. Not all that we may meet are gentle, kind or have our best interests in mind.

Some people have asked: "Aren't you afraid that teaching someone to journey without going with them will cause a problem?" No. Because we all have a power animal, at least one, who is watching over us all the time. You can bet that in All Time/No Time, which is the real world, your power animal knows when you are going to journey for the first time before you do. It will be there. But, you must ask to see it. In all this work, with the Powers, with guides, angels, power animals, you first must ask; that is a universal law. As Children of Earth & Sky, we are powerful beings; we were sent here for a purpose, and even if we don't recognize our purpose, and walk like cattle upon the Earth with our heads down to the ground, unconscious and unknowing, we still have higher powers that watch over us. It's up to us to recognize them and appeal to them to show themselves and help us.

It's very rare that a person does not have a power animal; occasionally, someone will come to me to retrieve one. But the symptoms of not having a power animal are very clear: if every imaginable thing that can go wrong goes wrong, repeatedly, it's likely you have lost your power animal or are between power animals. In that case, it may be useful to find a shaman and have him or her retrieve one for you by going into the lower world and finding one that is willing. It could be one from an earlier time, perhaps from youth, or one that is more pertinent to your current stage in life. If you journey, you will find it, too. You will know your power animal because it will appear to you from at least three vantage points, it will appear friendly and you will feel a kinship. If it shows teeth or fangs, or appears threatening or incites fear of any kind, it is not your power animal. It's like they say about falling in love: You'll know it when you see it.

Once you have connected with your power animal, or totem, in this way, pay homage to it: put pictures of the animal or being, or one like it, perhaps cut from a magazine or printed out from the Internet, on your refrigerator, or desk, or altar, or carry one around in your purse or pocket. Power animals are like stray cats, if you feed them, in this case, with heart-felt gratitude and appreciation, they tend to hang around. Also, read about the characteristics of the animal. Notice which qualities it possesses that you share, and which ones are qualities you desire, and ask the power animal to help you in these matters. You will be surprised what comes your way.

From the Energy Notebook: Reiki Guides Seen Shamanically

For those who practice Reiki but not shamanism, or vice versa, I can say that it's quite an experience to work with the Reiki guides in non-ordinary reality.

The first time I journeyed after receiving a Reiki attunement, I saw the Reiki guides as a gigantic pillar of purple, like a purple totem pole, with the faces of the guides stacked one atop the other seemingly stretching into eternity.

As I was marveling at this, my own Reiki guide appeared in a swirl of purple.

He took me into the purple pillar and I "became" Reiki energy.

It was as if I were looking through the eyes of a fly — a thousand facets.

If I moved forward, I could see through each facet, focus through one at a time, where hands were being placed on people for Reiki healing.

I "was" the energy. I couldn't see the whole body being worked on, but only the part where the hands were placed and my purple healing energy was flowing into that body.

If I pulled back, I could see the thousand facets again, as I floated in the purple pillar. Wherever people were laying on hands for healing, using the Reiki energy anywhere on the globe, I was a part of it.

It was very beautiful and timeless; I could have stayed there forever. But human time is much more limited than that of the spiritual beings and I had to return.

Since then, I've acquired several Reiki guides that often accompany me in my journeys and assist in healing in non-ordinary reality. They also appear in nightly dreaming, and transport me to people and places needing healing work.

Review

Healing through the shamanic journey:

- Recognize that everything is related, and has power in the now, which is eternal and connects all beings.

- Practice shamanic journeying, expanding your world.

- Allow yourself to be an agent of healing, practicing Reiki in the shamanic journey and in Dreamtime.

- Consistently thank your power animals, guides and the Creator.

Internet key words: *power animals, totems, non-ordinary reality, Akashic Field, Christ Consciousness Grid, Plume of Quetzalcoatl.*

Pathfinder Reiki Symbol

Null Point

Ending, completion, passing through ascension.

Chapter Four

Inner/Outer Journeys

*Shape your world through your light.
Illuminate your unique path. Don't live in the
shadow of others' judgments. They are not
yours — unless you let them be so.*

— ASCENSION TESTS

Being a Reiki shaman requires knowledge, both of this world and of other worlds. It's a movable feast of learning, for suddenly, the world is literally unbounded. As you begin, increase knowledge incrementally; start with basics, that is, practicing that which you know. Do the exercises and perform the applications. If you don't feel you have succeeded, try again later. There is no pressure here, no deadlines, no "get it right, right now." Learning is a process, sometimes a slow one, but one day you will discover that all that you once might have thought you couldn't do suddenly has become effortless. Forgive yourself, laugh if you fail, for you have not failed; you simply haven't reached where you think you ought to be. The more you journey, the more you learn, and your guides and power animals will help you. They can teach you far more than you could ever dream.

There are two essentials: *one,* to never leave on a shamanic journey without your power animal, and *two,* never undertake to practice healing on anyone without their permission.

One of my favorite stories happened a few years ago, involving my then-teenaged son, who lived with his mother in another city. We were both online and he "instant messaged" me he was having trouble with an ingrown toenail. Being a teenager, he was not always keen on letting his father know what he was up to, but apparently the toe was giving him such trouble that he asked for help. I asked if he wanted me to journey for him to work on his toe with Reiki and he readily agreed — but ONLY if that's ALL I did!

So I journeyed shamanically through the middle world and found him — with his power animals standing on each side of him looking stern, to ensure that working on his toe was all that I did. I performed a Reiki treatment and the next day he e-mailed that his toe was much better.

I still laugh at the image of the power animals. But, that's what they are there for, to serve and protect — and not let daddies, or anyone else, pry!

It does not matter if you are a father, son, husband, daughter, or any close or distant relation, you have no business trying to intervene in someone's healing process without their permission. As a matter of ethics, I have every person who requests healing from me to fill out a form. The form states the legal definition of complementary and alternative medicine so that there can be no question of the services being offered, and gives me permission to work on the person. Not only is this a basic prerequisite in today's litigious society, but it also serves the function of *asking* for help.[1] We all need help from time to time, but unless we ask for it, how can we expect to be helped? It's a universal principle, even among guides, angels, power animals, Creator, that unless we drop the ego enough to seek help, it's doubtful that we'll get it. That works for everyone. A friend who studied for a while with Fools Crow, the famed Lakota medicine man, related an instance of the elderly man catching pneumonia. Being young and naïve, my friend taunted, "How can you be such a powerful medicine man and be sick like that?" Immediately, he saw the foolishness of his question, and feeling remorse and shame, began to perform his own ceremonies to aid in the old man's recovery. The next day, Fools Crow was fine, as if nothing had happened, and my friend had learned a valuable lesson: No matter how "great" we may be, we are still humans inhabiting physical bodies. We all require the prayers of many and the grace of God.

In my own practice, I know better than to try to work on myself; it's the same as a doctor trying to remove his own gallbladder; it can't be done. And I've learned the utter futility of trying all but generalized Reiki and simple techniques for loved ones (like working on my son's toe). We're often too close to be objective and neutral, able to clearly hear the guides speak to us, or be accurate in discernment. We often hear what we want to hear. So, it's a good idea to teach others the techniques you have learned, and be willing to work on them, and have them work on you. It has to do with humility. Unless we are humble in the sight of Creator, He cannot see us to help us in our work. That, in essence, is being "the hollow bone."

As an example of this, at a Native American gathering a man came up to me and started boasting of all the shamanic things he could do, some of which were rather frightening. I just smiled and listened, friendly but not particularly interested. After a while, he went away, and my companion asked: "What was all that about?" I replied that the man was obviously trying to intimidate me with all his knowledge and power. "But aren't you afraid he will use it against you?" my friend asked. No, I replied, because I don't have any power. I am utterly powerless, and hence have no one but Creator to protect me.

My friend looked at me for a long moment, and then it dawned on him what I was saying. "With all that stuff in his head," I told my friend, "he's terribly limited. Creator is limitless. I know nothing and need to know nothing. Creator knows everything, and so I rely on Creator." That is being the hollow bone. If there is a lot of "stuff" cluttering up your head — whether it's Reiki stuff or shamanic stuff, or boasts or intricate formulas, or whatever — that clogs up the hollow bone. It is useful to know things, but only to the extent that you can open up to the miracles available and allow them to move through you. Personal power is always limited; Creator's Power is limitless.

Beyond the humility of asking permission, one must be open enough to receive it. We cannot intervene where we're not wanted. If someone clings too tightly to one's dis-ease so as not to release it, then there's nothing an outside agent can do. One of my first clients was a man who was confined to a wheelchair. I went to his house and only through talking with him learned that he didn't want to be healed, only healed enough so that he could enjoy himself while still receiving his disability check. I explained that not only could I not guarantee that he would be healed, due to the nature of holistic healing, but if he allowed healing to take place, it's possible he might be totally healed whether he liked it or not. He declined further assistance, given that he couldn't control the limits of his wellness.

We are also limited to asking permission by karma — the concern we noted earlier by the Tibetan orders of centuries ago that using Reiki for healing could disrupt the cycle of births. Interceding on one's behalf may not be welcome because a certain condition is that person's life choice or path. For example, had I not fallen out of the oak tree in 1992, I would probably not have pursued a healing path; had I not suffered excruciating, chronic, unremitting pain, I would probably not have developed the compassion to learn and share healing techniques; had not that path led me to a shamanism conference a Reiki master just happened to be attending, you wouldn't be reading this book. And so on. The terrible accident and pain dramatically changed my life for the better and led to the healing and relief of many.

Besides all this, it may be impossible for healing to occur without permission. For example, when I was starting my soul retrieval practice, a friend who started at the same time said she was having difficulty "seeing" a client in nonordinary reality. Confident, and without asking, I arrogantly said, "I'll bet that I can do it." My friend raised her eyebrows, but said nothing.

I went to the place I usually lie down to journey in my house, put on earphones for a drumming CD, and went to the place I always wait for my power animal. First my bear power animal came. I said that I wanted to go see what was going on with this person. My bear refused to take me. I was shocked. This had never happened before. So, I called on my owl power animal. The owl came. I repeated my request. My owl refused to take me. Now, I was getting irritated. I chastised them both: "You are power animals; you are supposed to serve me! Why are you not helping?" They said nothing. Exasperated, I called upon my eagle. My eagle power animal doesn't show up very often, usually only for an important lesson, or to signal that I must pay utmost attention. We waited and waited, the bear, owl and I at the entrance to the underworld, and finally my eagle showed up. I uttered my request for a third time. Wonder of wonders, and infuriatingly, my eagle refused.

"Very well, then," I exclaimed, disgusted. "I'll just go on by myself!"

Mind you, one never wants to go alone into nonordinary reality. While it's likely nothing will happen, there's the possibility that anything can happen, and it's simply imprudent. The power animal is your guide and protector, able to explain the inexplicable, protect you and get you out of a bind, if necessary. Before I could launch off on my own, my eagle turned around for me to hop onto its back and away we went. We traveled out across the middle world until we came to a neighborhood and began circling. I could make out each house, until I saw the house that the woman lived in. It was all shuttered with nails hammered on doors and windows and big signs reading: "Keep Out!" I asked my eagle to drop me off, and we landed in the yard. I tried walking across the lawn, but it was like trying to walk on very slippery mud, without any traction. Finally, I had to admit defeat, and I climbed on the back of my eagle and we returned. When I told my friend what had happened, she confirmed details of the woman's house and neighborhood, and that I had been in the right place, but took great delight that I had been unsuccessful in obtaining any useful knowledge, and only the little that I got because my power animals took pity on me and deemed it an important lesson to learn. "You didn't have permission to do any work," my friend rightly and appropriately pointed out. The message was received.

Since then, when people have asked me to check on someone, I relate this story. A couple of times, even after I had told of the difficulty of helping someone who hasn't asked for it, I've been persuaded to "check in" on someone, usually someone's child or loved one, and the lesson on the ethics of getting permission has been reinforced, though gently. For example, one of my best friends asked me to look in on her grown daughter who was ill, explaining that she didn't "believe in" complementary and alternative medicine and "wouldn't say yes to it." I journeyed to see what I could see. In the journey, her daughter seemed to be obscured by a blurry cloud, so I could see her outline but could not see what exactly was going on. Her power animal was standing over her, and I asked if there was anything I could do. It said I could send Reiki energy, which I did, directing the Reiki energy to the power animal who, in turn, directed it to my friend's daughter. I could see the Reiki energy, which usually appears to me as a purple radiance going to the power animal, where it was changed into golden energy that bathed her daughter.

Later, my friend told me that her daughter took a miraculous turn for the better, healing very quickly, and told her mom: "I know you were doing some of your mumbo jumbo for me. I could feel it! Thanks!" It just goes to show that we can pray for anyone, whether it's sending best wishes, fervent "get wells" or Reiki energy, in journey or not. It will be accepted, or not.

Ways of Journeying

It's normal for individuals to have various styles of journeying, but over the years I've developed a few standard ways. To just have a look around (and I highly recommend it, to get used to being with your power animal and just keeping in touch with things), it's useful to have a spot in your house you routinely use to journey. It could be a spare bedroom, or living room. For years, when I had an unused upstairs room, I would just plop down on the carpeted floor, put on a set of earphones (to block outside noise) and put on my drumming CD.[2] While journeying and drumming at the same time is doable with practice (and allows for more flexibility as far as the length of the journey), a CD is easier. It's also easier to jot down visions or communications immediately after the journey than to try to use a tape recorder during it. I used a tape recorder for a while, but noticed that there were long lapses, filled with a barrage of information too fast to speak, and attempting to say it all actually decreased the amount of information, rather than helping to retain it. I journey and then get up, go to my computer and write down as much as I can remember.

In this type of "looking around" journey, I'll let the drum start, then envision the place where I enter the lower world. That used to be the mouth of a big ceramic bear I had downstairs where I used to live; but that bear eventually crumbled and is long gone. The opening into the underworld can be anything: a crack in the floor, a hole in a tree in the yard, a culvert in the street, a cave you once visited, or even the hole in the sink — any opening going down that you can envision and feel that you can "connect."

Once there, I'll look for my power animal, my bear. If he doesn't show up immediately, I'll whistle for him, in a tone that he taught me. He'll usually show up. Then, we'll either go up into the upper world, or down into the lower world; rarely, out into the middle world. Unless I have something specific I want to know or a place I want to go, where we go or what we do is pretty much up to my power animal.

When doing work for someone, such as retrieving a soul part or power animal, it's useful to take this type of "look around" beforehand. I always do this, after a rather unsettling experience years ago. When I was first doing soul retrieval, a woman who had extensive shamanic experience asked me to do a soul retrieval long distance. Being new to it, and full of naïve arrogance, that is, utter ignorance, I plopped down on the floor and journeyed out to retrieve the soul piece. Little did I know that the woman had somehow in the course of her journeys become the enemy of three witches — *bruja* of the Sonora Desert — who had stolen her soul parts. I wandered right in to their abode, saw her soul pieces as if bound in chains and cut the chains without thinking. As the soul parts were released, the witches turned on me. Luckily, in the blink of an eye, my power animal intervened and the next thing I knew, I was spinning way out in the void somewhere.

The psychic attacks and battles with the witches went on for weeks; which, actually was good, for it taught me what to do in such an event, how to do it, and so forth.[3] But I learned a valuable lesson: whenever doing work for someone, scope out the situation first. Now I always peek ahead to see what is required before I commit to doing any journey work (after getting permission, of course). It's a precaution, and it actually works to both of our advantage. When someone contacts me, I ask the person to fill out my Client Request Form, then, with permission, I'll take a gander at what's up. Then I report back. The client takes it from there: we either do the work, or not.

This is helpful in that if a client wants work to be done, I already know what is to be done and the actual work can be done quickly. For example, here's a sample of a report I will have written and sent to them, along with what was told to me that needed to be done.

Notes From A Typical Client Journey

Date
Journey for Annabelle Client
Went to my bear cave and met my bear.
We went down into the underworld and went to a place where there were woods; a very green glade. I asked, "Are we looking for a power animal?" Bear answered "yes."
I looked around; it was an incredibly vivid place; trees, growing things. I looked and there through the trees came a white object, and gold glowing things around it.
It came closer and I saw it was a unicorn. Brilliant white; the feeling was of such love and purity, innocence, it blew me away.
The golden orbs around it were fairies and angels.... All manner of powers.
I looked around and the whole glade was alive with these bright spirit beings.... Elves, fairies, little people, fireflies that had their own love and wisdom.
It was an incredible place; I didn't want to leave.
But this was just a scouting expedition.
I was told the unicorn was to be Annabelle's power animal. The other magical creatures would go where the unicorn went. The unicorn would lead Annabelle to the youth and innocence that she lost, if she would allow the unicorn to do so.
Although I didn't want to leave, it wasn't my place to linger, so we journeyed up, toward the upper world. My guides wanted me to go into the middle world.... To go look at some other things.... Not related to Annabelle, but I told them I was on a mission here, for Annabelle, so we went up to the upper world.
We didn't have to travel too far.

I saw ahead a huge white light; huge. I couldn't make out anything, just blinding light. So I asked my Bear to help; I changed perspectives and saw that it was revolving energy, that looked like a spiral galaxy. It was from her childhood; lots of energy.

Around it, I saw many satellites, like smaller round galaxies attached to the huge spiral galaxy. Bear said these are all soul pieces that were spun off in childhood, at different times, that have gravitated together.

I asked how I was to implant them all; Bear said that I should blow in the central soul piece in the large galaxy and the rest would follow.

There are more pieces that are further out, I was told, but they would come in, in time, on their own accord once the large one is implanted.

I asked if there was more and I was told, no. This is enough. We went to the Sky Lodge, the place where I do my long distance work and I looked at Annabelle's energy body. It looked like a white tornado, drawing in energy through the heart and crown.

I was told that I was not to do any work on her at this time. Later, maybe.

I saw Reiki guides and angels. She is well attended.

I asked if there was anything else, and was told no.

I returned home..

Aho.

Work:

1 Power animal: a unicorn

1-plus Soul parts: spiral and associated pieces.

The in-person healing journey

If you have performed an exploratory journey for someone who wants help in person, then you would go to your usual spot, lay out a blanket, and have the person lie down. When you are ready, you lie next to the client, shoulder to shoulder, while the drum takes you where you need to go.

For example, I usually have the person lie down, then I will rattle and smudge the area (spreading sacred smoke, such as cedar or white sage to cleanse the air, or using liquid smudge), walking around four times to make a sacred circle, then drumming for a while to get ready to launch into a journey.[4] When I'm ready, I'll quit drumming and either have someone drum or use a CD to continue in the journey. (My wife will often drum for me, if the client doesn't object. Doing shamanic work for someone like this can be a very personal event; so the client may want someone close to be there, or may want the opposite, to have no friends or family present. Either way is fine with me. Generally, I believe it's a good idea to have a person of the opposite gender with you when you do this work if working with the opposite sex, so the client will feel comfortable. Energy work does not involve touching, it is done fully clothed, and is not at all sexual — but allowing someone to work on your energy body requires trust — so it is important to respect the client's wishes in this matter). I'll lie down next to the person, put a cloth over my face, hold my crystal to my chest, and go out into nonordinary reality.

In this example with Annabelle Client, I would go into the underworld, blow the power animal into the small hand-held crystal I use for this work, go to the upper world, blow the soul part into the crystal, and then return and blow the energetic pieces from the crystal into Annabelle's heart chakra, then help her sit up, and blow them down her crown chakra. Then, I would help her lie back down, remove any spiritual intrusions there may be by pulling them out with my hands and tossing them into a bowl of water (I have a special healing bowl I use this for; water neutralizes energy; just pour the water outside when you are through) and do a brief Reiki treatment on the person, smoothing out the aura, implanting mental/emotonional symbols in it for healing and protection, and putting the Hon she ze sign over the crown so that Reiki energy will be released in doses in coming days.

The long-distance healing journey

Sometimes, all a person needs is a Reiki treatment and the removal of spiritual intrusions, and often this can be done long distance. If so I journey to The Sky Lodge, and do Reiki on the person, removing intrusions. In The Sky Lodge, it should be noted, I "see" the person as if scrying, that is, as if in a crystal ball. What I'm doing looks like that scene in *The Wizard of Oz* where the wicked witch and her flying monkey are looking in the crystal ball and cackling about Dorothy and her little dog, except that it's quite beautiful there in the upper world, just beyond the Christ Consciousness Grid, with the Earth a beautiful blue-and-white globe suspended in space in the background. It's as if I have a small, open cabin there with a little manger where I can look down at the body of the person who I'm working on. The body does not appear as a physical body, but as an energetic outline; usually spokes going outward from the central core, with the arms and legs as slightly more substantial lines of golden energy. I can see dark areas where there are intrusions or blockages, and can see where energy may be weak and need to be burnished more brightly. I will hold my hands over this outline of energy as if doing a Reiki treatment on a physical body, implanting Reiki symbols, if or where necessary, and smoothing out lines of energy so that all flows smoothly and it glows more brightly. While doing this, my power animal(s) and Reiki guide(s) are there gently advising, instructing and directing. No action is taken unless the guides prescribe it.

Notes From Long-Distance Work

Date
Journey for Annabelle Client
Went to my bear cave and met my bear; we went to the underworld to see if Anabelle needed a power animal; was told that she did. Saw any number of them eager to be her power animal. Was finally shown one, a bird, some type of water bird. At first, I thought it was an albatross. Or perhaps one of those skimmer birds you see on the beach. But was told that it was a fulmar.
I blew the bird into my crystal and headed toward the upper world.
As I was passing through the Christ Consciousness grid to the upper world, I was met by an angel-like being. Was told that

he would act as a guide or power animal for her, also. He appeared like a golden wisp, but had the power of the Earth; which is why he was on the Earth side of the CC grid. I proceeded to The Sky Lodge.

There, I looked down at Annabelle's energy body. There were angels all around her, everywhere. She is surrounded by angels and guides of various types, including Reiki guides. (Has she taken Reiki?? If not, she should; that is, they are there, should she choose to use them.) She appeared as if golden streamers were hanging off of her. I saw that the golden streamers are attachments to her place, where she is, how she is, and that is holding her back (streamers that had turned dark and ugly, sickly). It appeared to me that the sickly ones need to be removed, so her assemblage points (which create her world) can be shifted.

I was told that, yes, she did need a soul part. So, my bear took me out further into the upper world and we found it. It appeared as a letter, an envelope. I was told that many years ago when she was in her teens or early 20s, she shed the energy, soul part, to carry the fear away; but the energy left, the fear remained. I was told that this soul part is a missing piece, to give her courage back, not fear. I was told: "It is permission." Permission to do what her heart tells her to do.

So, I went back to The Sky Lodge, and I blew the soul part and the bird power animal and the spirit to her. I saw them locate within her and anchor in her energy body, so she has them within and without.

I was told that the bird would range far and wide and would guide her to where she needs to go, if she will listen to his voice.

I was told that she could call on the golden spirit to move obstacles from her path. His is with her, as is the spirit bird.

They are all now there to help her.

But, still, I looked at her energy body as it appeared to me, with the sickly attachments and I thought maybe I ought to cut them and set her free. My bear said, no, that only she could undo the attachments and it would be wrong of me to do it; besides, it might cause harm. Her body looked like a medicine drum with the streamers attached; I was told: "Only she can beat her drum."

I looked around and on the other side of the drum, I found an obsidian knife. It was small, about 6 inches long, but very sharp. "See," my bear said, "she has the tool to cut herself free."

But I was told that she was afraid to use it. It would hurt someone; maybe someone that she is not consciously aware of, though her inner wisdom knows. With the permission (soul part), she can make the choice to let the attachments go, without cutting them; they will simply wither into nothing and detach.

I did some Reiki work on her; there were a few spiritual intrusions that were removed; I implanted a guide symbol in her crown chakra to help her see with clarity, to help her see where Spirit leads, and some other work

Then, that was all.

Cameback.

Aho.

A World of Worlds

Now that you have learned how to journey and have started practicing, be aware that there is a world of worlds out there, more than can be imagined.

There are other levels or planes of existence and other universes, including one where everything is in two dimensions, which is quite an interesting experience, and another that I call "the crack in the universe," through which souls go after death.

Ordinarily, the crack in the universe is off limits to journeying. It's way, way out and hard to get to, but I have seen my own death while journeying and have traveled through it and back; though it was so beautiful on the other side, I really didn't want to return.[5]

I have had to journey for people who have had soul parts lodged there. Since they were still alive, the pieces couldn't pass through. In one journey, I found a soul part of the client that had been stolen by her deceased father. He had always criticized her in life, never recognizing her achievements, always expressing disappointment and anger toward her. When he passed on, he saw the error of his ways and refused to cross over until he could return the stolen energy. So, he stayed lodged there, his spirit body on the other side, his hands on this side holding a golden globe of soul essences.

She had felt the loss in her life and came to me, not knowing what was wrong, but knowing something was "missing" in her life. So, when I journeyed, I was taken to this place, where I retrieved the missing soul pieces and returned them to her, making her whole and also allowing her father to cross over.

That helping to the Afterlife is called psychopomp and it often is encountered while journeying. The first time I did psychopomp, I was journeying on a scouting mission for retrieving a soul part for a client and was told by my guides that I was needed elsewhere on a matter of greater importance. I was taken to the site of a plane crash off the coast of California (I didn't know exactly where the crash was until sometime later when I saw it on the news) and I saw the souls of several of those who had died hovering over the water. They were very elongated, appearing to be looking down at the fragments of their physical bodies which were still unrecovered from the ocean. My drumming gave them strength to let go and move toward the light.

Since then, I've done it many times, most notably on September 11, 2001, when I went into the middle world to the site of the World Trade Center on the night of the tragedy. I traveled just below the upper world; and saw the grid separating the upper world from the Earth (the Christ Consciousness Grid/Plume of Quetzalcoatl). It was extremely unstable and bright from all the souls released by the event and humankind's global intent powering it up through prayer and emotion.

At the site, I saw the bright lights and dust still hanging as in the TV pictures; but I could not see the human rescuers. They were like ghosts, blurred. The souls of the dead were like live bodies, in sharp focus. Many of the souls were standing around dazed or wandering around; most I saw were curled up like they were asleep. They didn't want to see their surroundings or acknowledge their reality. There were beings from other dimensions observing; some helping.

I tried alternating my drumming through my heart and crown chakras to orient them toward the light. Energy from my crown chakra was shooting up into the light. I saw many go toward the light along my drumming; but many more either wouldn't get up or wake up or were wandering aimlessly. I spoke to many. So many souls were there, in various states of dazed and confused awareness: it was overwhelming.

That was the first night. The second night was easier. I drummed and my helping spirits met me there, where they had stayed behind. They were ministering to the dead and dying. I got to stay pretty much in my body, at interface with one of my helping spirits who showed me through his eyes what was going on. My drumming gave power to them and provided an impulse toward the light, from Earth energy toward the Christ Consciousness Grid. I was both there and at home in consciousness at the same time; able to ground better and hold a beacon of drumming light toward the light stable.

The third evening, I rested. Each day I had worked and each evening I had drummed, and then continued the healing work while sleeping, working all night in my dream state helping souls toward the light; so that I was feeling exhausted.

Interestingly, each morning when I awoke, I felt as if I were covered in dust, my face and hands thick with it. Each morning in the shower I had to wash this chalky, dry energetic debris off of me.

As I went to bed the third night, I prayed: "Please, Creator, angels, guides, helping spirits, let me rest tonight," as I was very tired. But a familiar voice full of gentle love and light said: "We need you. Can't you come?"

And I smiled just before drifting off and said, "yes."

I awoke the next day covered in dust again.

After about two weeks, the visits in Dreamtime slowed, as I left my helping healing deer spirits to do the work and I checked on them from time to time. It was an emotional time for everyone, on heaven and earth.

Odd Journeys Are Not Only Possible, But Probable

You never know where you might end up during a journey. Some of the experiences are quite profound, heart-wrenching, as in the aftermath of the psychopomp of 9/11; others are just plain odd.

For example, once I asked my power animal if there was anything I needed to know (thinking: non-ordinary reality) and I was taken through the Internet. I guess you would call it a middle-world journey because instead of going to the "hole" where I usually enter, my power animal took me downstairs and into my computer (which was logged on) and off we went! Zip! Zip! Zip! I saw mostly offices, with people working. Some of the offices were empty, so I just looked around at papers on the desks and empty coffee cups, etc. I found perceiving through the computer very fractured, disjointed. There were many images at once and they had to be pieced together, as with a stack of transparencies, and they shifted and changed. So, you might be looking at 10 places at once. You only get a second to glimpse one spot before you're looking at and actually being in another. You're "at" a bunch of places at the same time, but you can only perceive a few at a time, so they flick in and out of sight. It's very energetically discombobulating, to say the least!

At one place, an empty office, big, with lots of desks, the overhead lights were out, but it was still light enough to see as another part of the office's lights were on. I was able to wander around in there for a moment and kept coming back to it; don't know why. I had the feeling there was something illegal going on in that place, involving electronic transfers of money.

At another place, there were two men and a woman, huddled over something, discussing it; some papers were spread out on a desk; they were very intense. They all had dark hair; the men with close-cropped hair, 30-ish; the woman with shoulder length hair, maybe 40. Whatever they were looking at was very important, under deadline; it meant a lot of money to them.

I had the feeling that the reason the scenes were shifting so fast and all at once was because the places I was visiting had computers that were logged on to the Internet constantly, through DSL, or a committed line. There were so many messages being sent and through so many ways that it made the signals chaotic, and therefore difficult to hold in intent and consciousness in any one place. That was a real "trip," so to speak. My advice to people who don't want people with shamanic ability snooping on them is: turn off your computer! While it would take a great deal of "want to" for someone to spy through a computer shamanically, since the routes and images are so chaotic, it's possible, as my power animal showed me in this journey.

Another time I asked my power animal if there was anything I needed to know and I was taken to a series of hallways deep in a mountain. It looked like a hospital of some kind, with grey/green walls. People were lying on gurneys, but they weren't dead. They were in some sorts of suspended animation, journeying themselves. As I watched, I saw a man in a lab coat standing over one of the bodies turn and look directly at me; he saw me in nonordinary reality. He did something I couldn't see, like turning a knob, and the vision went blank. It came to me later that this was some kind of government experiment on distant viewing.

The worlds of non-ordinary reality appear differently to different people, but they have general areas of agreement similar to all cultures. An aborigine in Australia and a modern American in New York could find many areas in common in non-ordinary reality. For example, mountains look like mountains, rivers like rivers, etc. But the symbols are likely to be different, since different symbols mean different things to different cultures. For example, when on a fast in Hopi country, I saw kachinas; one I recognized as an Egyptian deity. Later, I realized that I recognized it as an ancient Power of Egypt because I had seen it depicted in a book; but to indigenous people in the area, without access to that book, it appeared as something else. The kachina appeared to me in a way that I could more accurately understand its powers and be familiar with it in a way of being friendly and approachable. I had seen it before, recognized it, and felt comfortable seeing it and relating with it. It's the same being, whether it appears as a crocodile to an Egyptian or a deer with a long snout to desert people.

In nonordinary reality, everything is symbolic; it's all symbols. That's why it is important to write down everything when doing a journey for someone. The symbols may mean nothing to you, but could mean a great deal to someone else. For example, once when doing a soul retrieval for a woman, one of the first images was in a bathroom where I saw a blue toothbrush and a red toothbrush. When I came out of the journey, I added that detail to my account, though it meant nothing to me, and it could have "meant" anything. One could be tempted to try to speculate or project meaning onto a vision like that, but I have learned through experience, that it's best to just write it down and relate it; it may mean something to the client. In this case, when I told the woman what I saw, she immediately started weeping. It turns out that her deceased husband used the red toothbrush; that is how they had them arranged and I had described the bathroom in their former house perfectly. By having this vision at the beginning, my guides were telling her that I was on track and legitimate and to pay attention; though it meant absolutely nothing to me.

Your guides will also use symbols to not only convey information, but play little jokes on you, as well. Another time, when just beginning soul retrieval work, I was asked to do a soul retrieval for a lady's cat. She had written asking if I could help, and I thought, well, I can try. I had never done healing work for an animal (but have done many since then), and ventured out not knowing what I would find. I saw the cat curled up on a calendar. The cat told me that it didn't need soul retrieval, but that it hated the food it was given, showing me the can that it didn't like and the kind that it did. Since the cat couldn't read, the cans appeared as bright colors; the hated one, mostly blue and green, the good one red and gold. I wrote all this down after the journey, but realized as I was writing that I didn't know the cat's name. I had journeyed for "Jane's cat." Oh, well, I thought, and went ahead and wrote it out. As I related this to the woman on the phone, I told her it was curled up on a calendar and she interrupted me: "What month was it?" she asked. "April," I replied. The woman started laughing. The cat's name was April. It was my guides showing me — and client — that I had the right cat — and reminding me in a humorous way that I had forgotten an important piece of information!

It is important that with any kind of journey work, we must act on what we see in nonordinary reality. As noted, when journeying, all is symbols. That is how the Divine beings communicate with us. They cannot operate on the physical plane, but we can. We can become the bridge for them through shamanism. Just as guides, power animals and angels can do healing work in nonordinary reality for us, we can perform miracles guided by them in this plane by moving the energy of their ideas through the human medium. It is in making these dreams into reality that we become who we were meant to be: children of Earth and Sky, cocreators with Creator, bringing heaven to earth, and healing the earth and ourselves.

Using Crystals in Your Practice

The effects of Reiki symbols are magnified and shamanic activities may be greatly enhanced by incorporating natural quartz crystals into one's practice.[6]

Many Native American medicine men view those who handle crystals derisively, since all "grandfathers," or stones, have powerful properties that in the hands of someone who knows how to use them are quite specific and effective.[7] They wonder: why would someone want to carry such a powerful stone? Although quartz crystals throughout time were carried by Cherokee priests and elders for healing and divination (often in adjudicating who was right or wrong in a dispute), there is generally a bias against carrying them, or at least displaying them openly. Such displays could even been seen as a threat. Some of the most powerful crystals in time have been secretly handed down, or even destroyed lest they find their way into the wrong hands, by native peoples. Some are so legendary they have their own names, and histories. In the hands — or even in the field of intent or aura — of someone who can manipulate healing energy, a crystal is a very powerful device indeed.

The reason is due to the form and structure of quartz crystals and the form and structure of the human body. An easy way to understand it is to see how crystals are used in electronics. Almost every electronic device uses a tuned circuit in one form or another for which a quartz crystal is naturally adapted. Although frequency synthesizers have replaced crystals in many applications, crystals are still used to filter, produce and modify electromagnetic signals.

The scientific name for quartz is silicon dioxide, rendered as SiO_2. Computers work because of silicon (providing the nickname "Silicon Valley" in California), derived from quartz crystals. The modern personal computer can be construed as a rather complicated crystal ball.

All minerals have highly ordered internal atomic structures with a regular geometric form. But a quartz crystal not only has that, but its internal form is expressed in its outward form. Each quartz crystal is a unique expression of its pure molecular makeup.

The power of the crystal is its piezoelectric effect — the natural property of crystals to amplify minute electric charges. Quartz crystals have a permanent electric polarization. If a quartz crystal is inserted into an electric field, the resulting stress changes its dimensions and amplification of the charge, in some cases many hundreds of times. So, whatever charge is applied to a crystal — mechanically or the human aura — is magnified. And it is magnified uniquely by the structure and composition of that crystal. So, different crystals — with eight faces or five or six — have different, unique properties for those who know how to use them in healing work.

Further, crystals have transmutational effects, meaning the crystals can easily change forms of energy as they are expressed. For example, any piezoelectric material, such as a quartz crystal, can convert a high-frequency alternating electric signal into an ultrasonic wave of the same frequency (changing an electric current into sound). They can produce ultrasound, which is sound with a frequency far higher than is audible to the human ear — above 20 kilohertz. Or a crystal can convert a mechanical vibration, such as sound, into a corresponding electrical signal (alternating voltage). So, sound can turn into an electric charge using a crystal or vice versa.

Hence, a crystal can be considered the most highly efficient and most versatile transmutation device of energy known to humankind. And it is all natural, produced by the Earthly Mother, perfect as it is. The highest science of today, working with ceramics and alloys sandwiched together, has not outdone the natural quartz crystal in electronics.

So, how does this relate to the human body? If we were to consider the human body in terms of its electromagnetic functions as an energy system, like a computer, we could accurately describe it as a living matrix, which has various properties as a dynamic solid state communication network. As a system of information exchange, the human body has both inward dynamics (regulating heart, lungs, thought, etc.) and external dynamics (the aura, composed of the various vortices of the chakras and layers of emotional, mental, etc., bodies).

The Human Body Is Like A Crystal

The body has been called a "tissue tensegrity-matrix system" or "the living matrix" in an attempt to describe its living/electrical function.

Like a crystal, the body can convert mechanical energy to electrical energy and vice versa as piezoelectric effects. By flexing muscles, for example, the body transmits electric signals between the muscles and the brain; it converts electrical to photonic (electric charges from the eyes to the brain) and back.

Like crystals, the human body has semiconductor properties, but it is more: it is a network of interrelated systems each with semi-conductor properties like a computer.

Like a computer using crystals, the body can produce coherent self-sustaining oscillations with complex harmonics.

Like a computer, the body can function as a solid state device that is capable of filtering, receiving, switching, storing and interpreting a wide array of signals, as well as reconfiguring, combining, splitting, amplifying and sending a wide array of signals.

So, the properties of the crystal are perfectly aligned with the energetic system of the body.

Together, in the same field, the body and a quartz crystal produce one interrelated system. By holding a crystal or even focusing intent on a crystal, the subtle energies of the body are amplified and/or transmuted. And these wonderful energy magnifiers are given freely to us by the Earthly Mother.

In fact, all Earth stones have healing properties based on their individual makeup. Some are more efficient, such as crystals. Each crystal is unique and has a distinctive shape; no two are exactly alike. But many have similar qualities in their application for healing therapy work. Some have the innate configuration to help deal with fears and anger. Some are better at centering or balancing or enhancing certain gifts.

With crystals, size doesn't matter. A big crystal doesn't have any "bigger" energy. Large crystals are good for using in medicine circles and meditation spots, though crystal clusters, quartz aggregates with a myriad of points, seem to work better in transmitting group energy. Crystals don't have to be perfectly clear to be "more" powerful, either. Clarity is an indication of male and female energies in the crystal. Neither is more powerful than the other and mixtures are especially beautiful. People who want perfectly clear or "museum quality" crystals are usually people who do not know the energy qualities of crystals, preferring what they think is considered of value. They are judging crystals as if they were diamonds, which they are not. The milky white quality represents the Ying or female side and the clear quality represents the Yang or male side of the crystal. Some perfectly white crystals are extremely powerful and certain "imperfections," or intrusions into the crystal matrix where it formed around another mineral, can be useful in accessing other qualities, such as those of the mineral encompassed, and magnifying those properties.

Broken or fractured crystals that have healed are particularly useful as healing crystals, and stones that are healing themselves provide an invigoration of healing energy within whoever carries the stone, for it is human energy passing through the stone that heals it, which magnifies the human host's own healing energy. For years, I carried a "broken" stone that when I found it was ragged and rough, but over time, using it in ceremony, it healed all its rough and broken parts and the fractures became beautiful features that reflected rainbows. The healing energy of Reiki accelerated not only the healing of the people who were exposed to the stone while it was used with them, but its own healing, as well — not to mention my own spiritual healing, growth and development!

Crystals can be powerful and useful even as fragments. Crystal fragments can be used in rattles (though they should be buffered with soft substances, such as the gourd's seeds to keep from tearing through the outer layer) for a particularly powerful ceremony. For thousands of years, medicine men have used crystals in translucent dried leather rattles at night because, when rattled, they produce light. Tiny crystal points in glasses, on shelves or windowsills help to provide a barrier to negative energy from entering a house. They brighten any room. Crystals in a bedroom promote more lucid dreaming. Carrying a crystal in your purse or pocket will cause you to ground frequently and become more aware, to be centered, and appreciate the energies at any moment.

Many people seem to like wearing a crystal on a necklace or thong. They are beautiful, but they should be cleansed often with running water or sunlight, so they don't become stuck in one energy pattern. It is better to have an array of crystals to choose from each day. Each day presents a different set of challenges and some crystals are more adept at, say, creativity rather than concentration, grounding, or receiving wisdom and direction. The right crystal for the day will present itself and some crystals are more versatile than others. They will know what your day will be before you do, so let them choose. Just become clear and feel your intuition. Even if you are anticipating an easy, routine day, if the crystal you usually carry to "punch through" hard times says it wants to accompany you that day, follow its advice. Rainbow crystals, particularly, provide light and magical energy to a day, but when times are troubled, they can be especially powerful in dispersing negative energy and keeping the heart warm. On good days they are a delight; on bad days, they can lighten the load to remind you that the blocks or setbacks are lessons, not punishments, and even great beauty and joy can be found in the darkest adversity.

As one becomes more attuned to energy, it will become easily apparent when a crystal needs to be set in the sun or put under running water or, even, set out in the moonlight. Crystals speak through intuition.

Additionally, those who work with energy will find that metal ornaments and jewelry will become uncomfortable if worn for any length of time. A good way to clear metal is to put the jewelry in a glass filled with crystal points to diffuse the energy so it can radiate back into the universe.

Some unusual configurations of crystals can be extremely powerful and even dangerous in the wrong hands. Laser crystals, for example, can be used by shamanic practitioners to seal off property from intruders, draw energy fields to cause bad intent to rebound on whoever aims it in that direction, and send extremely focused energy wherever aimed. It would be a bad idea, for example, to "point" a laser crystal at someone and even jokingly say "drop dead."

But crystals themselves are technically neutral; they amplify the intent and karmic influence of whoever holds them. For good karma, carry crystals and give them to whoever wants or needs one. Hold out a handful and say, "pick one." You'll be surprised not only at the delight of the receiver, but also at the selection. Ones that you think are particularly pretty, even valuable monetarily, will often be ignored for that special one that lights up the chooser's eyes. Remember: No matter what the size, color, clarity or monetary worth, crystals don't belong to you. They belong to the Earthly Mother and are gifts to be lovingly cherished and freely given. One of the best ways to get to know crystals is to dig them yourself.[8]

The best test for finding the right crystal for you is simply to be drawn to it. No one "owns" a crystal. We only hold them for a while. Crystals pick us and then when it's time to help someone else, they go to them. You will know when it's time to give away your crystal, for it will just leap into your hand and into the hand of someone else. Or, it will just "disappear."

Crystals appear and disappear all the time. You can keep a crystal in a prominent place, say on your mantle, and it will one day be gone. Days or weeks may go by and one day, there it will be, right where it's supposed to be. Or, it will turn up somewhere else where you'll think, "hmmm, that's where I would have put it, if I were going to put it somewhere."

That's just one of the quirks of crystals. They phase in and out of ordinary reality, or "realm shift," as it's called. They actually create portals in time and space from which to shift here, there, wherever. The crystal that I used to help so many people realm shifted, once, for nine months. I put it on the table where I always put it and next time I looked, it was gone. Nine months later, there it was, right where I had put it.

In the higher teachings of Reiki, practitioners are taught to build crystal grids to hold intent, especially useful in therapeutic massage under a table when working on a client with a particularly troublesome or chronic condition.

When receiving a crystal from anyone, it is best to wash it, let it sit in the sun or bury it for a few days to remove any latent patterns. Some crystals collect and hold patterns more than others.

Crystals are especially powerful when used in rattles for sacred ceremonies. They break up environmental energy very well in any setting, cleansing the energy field and recharging ambient energy.

When choosing crystals at a digging site, you should state your intent for them and ask which ones want to go. Crystals will tell you if they want to go with you or stay on the mountain. If you glimpse one and then it disappears no matter how hard you look, leave it behind. Don't search for it. It's not for you.

Conversely, a crystal may "pop out" from a pile of rocks or within dense vegetation; it may even appear on a heavily traveled footpath and you'll wonder, "how did anyone miss that one?" That crystal obviously is signaling it is meant to go with you.

To someone who doesn't deal with crystals much, this may sound crazy. But, if you work with them as a Reiki shaman, you'll discover that crystals are truly living rocks. All rocks hold energy and all rocks have "life," of a sort, as even the quantum physicists can attest. Each has properties and varying degrees of vibratory value.

But, crystals are special. They truly are eternal gifts of the Earthly Mother freely given from her bountiful heart, as beautiful as diamonds, but much more plentiful, and filled with good vibrations.

Most crystals are just happy-go-lucky little rock beings of light and love wanting to be filled with human energy to beam out into the universe.

They light up our lives.

And they are perfect for the healing power of Reiki.

Other Modalities

As a Reiki Shaman, you should be aware of other energy modalities, though it is not necessary to be proficient in them. All doors lead to the same room; one modality is not "better than" or "worse than" another, though some seem more efficacious than others for particular issues.

Most of the body work techniques available today are variations of Qigong, the Chinese art more than 2,500 years old of cultivating internal energy.

The various techniques, which include acupuncture, shiatsu, Tai Chi, Reiki and others, can be divided into three categories: 1) improving health; 2) improving martial arts; 3) achieving spiritual enlightenment.

Qigong is itself an offshoot of Chinese traditional medicine. Developed over the course of more than 5,000 years, traditional Chinese medicine is a wellspring of vibrational medicine systems being used in the West today. The system is unique for its diagnostic methods, pharmacology and treatment, including acupuncture, deep breathing and therapeutic use of massage.

Chinese medicine is based on the theories of yin (negative) and yang (positive) forces which can be seen as the male and female principles of the Earth spirituality, and of the five elements: metal, wood, water, fire, and earth. And it holds as its centerpiece the appreciation and manipulation of Chi (or Qi) or life force energy.

In traditional Chinese medicine every thing or every phenomenon in the universe consists of two forces, yin and yang, that oppose each other and at the same time complement each other.

In the universe, in the Oriental belief of Tao, everything is composed of complementary forces. So, the human body must comply with universal law, as well. When there is a balance, there is no dis-ease. With imbalance comes illness or dis-ease. Hence, the whole body must be treated.

In Chinese medicine, the human body is divided into organ systems, each with their own functions that do not necessarily relate to the organs literal placement and functions. Each organ corresponds with the five elements. So, prescriptions would be a mix of air and fire and so forth for treatment of dis-ease corresponding with the patient's body, personality type, demeanor and other physical aspects and psychological predisposition. Treatments are designed specifically for each individual, so that even if two people have the same symptoms, they might receive different treatments. Treatments use natural herbs extensively, as well as a prescribed diet for certain chronic conditions or dispositions.

Eastern thought predominates in alternative medicine modalities, which can include traditional Chinese medicine, applying ancient wisdom of the Hindu Vedas, Indian Yogic and Ayurvedic medicine.

New methods for incorporating mind/body techniques with spiritual principles are being developed every year, with ever more now being trademarked by practitioners. The great duty of people today, to facilitate healing and wholeness of the Earth, is to seek to understand and use whatever healing systems work for the individual and not discourage or disparage any truly helpful alternative medical model.

In all the emerging modalities, the patients are also the health care providers. We truly do heal ourselves by practicing these health care alternatives. Teachers are students and students are teachers. There is no outside "authority." The "authority" is within, through the inherent wisdom of the body. No one can impose wellness on anyone and to say that someone is a health care "provider" is something of a misnomer both in traditional and alternative medicine. In order to be healed, one must want to be healed. And, like being "a little bit pregnant," wellness cannot be parceled out.

Entire books have been and are being written on these healing technologies, and the growth and development of new modalities is so dramatic, it would be impossible to detail them all. But a brief synopsis of some of the new and old modalities regarding body work, health and the spirit is in order, since Reiki, shamanism and Reiki shamanism are allied with them under the category of alternative energy medicine and share many characteristics. Look around you. There are new modalities and practitioners of ancient systems blossoming everywhere. As a practitioner of "energy medicine," being a Reiki shaman, you should be at least cognizant of other modalities, some of which you may wish to pursue. Here are a few that have achieved some level of acclaim or popularity in Western culture:

Therapeutic Touch

Therapeutic Touch is probably the most well-known energy therapy using the concepts of Polarity Therapy that is accepted by the medical community today, at least in hospitals. It was developed in the early 1970s by Dolores Krieger, Ph.D., R.N., then professor of Nursing at New York University.

Working with Dora Kunz, a "natural" healer, they developed a form of "hands-on" healing which can be easily taught and easily learned and it is used in many hospitals today. It is similar to Reiki in its application but it does not require an attunement. In Therapeutic Touch, the hands gently smooth and shape the aura and specific energy points can be messaged with very little pressure. For many in the medical profession, Therapeutic Touch and its related Healing Touch (developed by Janet Mentgen, a nurse who has used energy-based care in her practice in Colorado since 1980) are as close as they will come to energy work as it is being practiced by body workers and spiritual healers. More than 100,000 patients in hospitals have been "touched" by these TTs or "touch therapies," as they are called, including Reiki, where nurses routinely practice these modalities.

The National Institutes of Health classifies Healing Touch as a "biofield therapy" because its effects are thought to be a result of manipulation of energy fields around the body. NIH notes on its Web site that energy medicine is gaining popularity in the marketplace and is now being studied at several academic medical centers.[9] Practitioners cite TT's success in calming seriously and terminally ill patients and gently allowing them to learn their life lessons in a non-threatening way in the harsh and sometimes physically hostile clinical environment. Those who practice TTs in the often less-than-sympathetic hospital environment are the pioneers of introducing energy medicine to countless numbers of suffering patients and their families, demonstrating that medical philosophies of wholeness and nurture have a benefit that is immeasurable.

Aromatherapy

Aromatherapy is derived from the ancient practice of using natural plant essences to promote health and well being. Scientists have long known that odors play an important part in the lives of animals. In the case of sex attractants, or pheromones, scent strongly influences animals to mate, bond, and nurture their offspring.

Scent is important to humans, too. Odors play a complex role in our lives, in the enjoyment of food, the attraction of one person to another, and in evaluating the cleanliness of our surroundings. The biochemical interaction between the molecules in the air and receptors inside the nasal passages triggers reactions in the brain.

The human nose has about 10 million olfactory nerve cells and one thousand different receptor types. Thus, the nose can detect odors of certain chemicals at better than 1 part per million, even better than most electronic devices. Most of what our noses detect is monitored beneath the level of consciousness and scents can play a powerful part in human behavior even if not appreciated consciously.

The reader of biblical texts will encounter mention of scented herbs and resins in various contexts, most commonly: cedar, cypress, hyssop, and cinnamon. But aromatherapy consists of the use of pure essential oils obtained from a wide assortment of plants, which have been steam distilled or cold-pressed from flowers, fruit, bark and roots. The essences are natural, not synthetic.

Aromatherapy can help ease a wide assortment of ailments, aches, pains, and injuries and the discomforts of many health problems. It also acts on the central nervous system, relieving depression and anxiety, reducing stress, relaxing, or uplifting and stimulating, depending on the essential oils being used, for general well being.

The essential oils taken from plants and used in aromatherapy are often selected for their "life force" — essential to the plants' biological process, as well as the substance that gives them their scent. Shamanically, a plant may give its Power in a way that may seem contraindicated. For example, if a plant with dark flowers calls to you, it may be signaling that it can take away dark thoughts or feelings, giving happiness, as opposed to a brightly colored plant that may seem to convey bright happiness on its surface. The essence of plants is often obscured by thinking of them in a left-brained or logical way.[12] Plant essences can be used in massage, combining their properties with the therapeutic power of touch. They can be used in baths as a simple, effective and pleasant way to relax and receive the therapeutic effects, or in compresses or through vaporization, as incense is used.

Homeopathy

Homeopathic medicine has been around for about 200 years and was invented by Samuel Hahnemann, a German doctor disillusioned by the medical profession of his day. He decided that healing is a rational, scientific process. His theory was that like cures like, that if a substance causes a particular reaction in a healthy person it can cure an unhealthy person with similar symptoms.

His theory has been greatly expanded during the intervening years to become one of the most popular and quickly growing modalities of healing. Homeopathy bridges the gap between vibrational medicine and medical science, in that it explores the proven relationships between natural substances including the wide array of herbal and non-herbal essences and treating the whole person in the tradition of Eastern thought.

Homeopathic medicine is a perfect adjunct to pharmacology, in that the substances used include diluted but highly "potentized" (as practitioners term it) agents drawn from nature, including minerals, metals, plants, animal and human disease products. Some are highly poisonous if taken in larger doses. But the dosages used in homeopathy are extremely minute, as much as 50,000-to-1.

How do such small concentrations work? That's not fully known, but two atoms colliding can create an atomic explosion; two atoms fusing can create a sun. Those principles were mysteries as far as practical application until the latter part of the 20th century, too.

Homeopathic medicine is widely practiced in France, where roughly 40 percent of the population uses it to treat everything from colds, flu and measles to depression, anxiety and insomnia. The same percentage of clinical physicians regularly use homeopathy in their practices, and the French government reimburses the cost of homeopathic medicines.

It does not have a stated spiritual component, being, as its founder intended, a scientific approach to healing — though a medicine man would note that all plants, animals and substances have Power, Creator's Power, or *nvwati* (Cherokee) good medicine, in them!

Many of the remedies can be found in health food stores in the United States, but they offer only a shotgun approach toward effecting a cure, more for crisis situations or broad-based symptoms rather than remedies crafted for the individual's particular needs. If given a choice, one should seek a reliable and successful homeopath for individual attention in order to receive an effective remedy.

Flower essences

Closely associated with homeopathy, but separate from it, is the use of flower essences to heal emotional/physical dis-ease. Flower essence therapy was founded by Dr. Edward Bach, an English homeopath, who in 1930 developed the system of natural remedies made from wildflowers. Like homeopathy, each plant remedy is aimed at addressing a specific state of mind that produces dis-ease. Flower essences are not drugs, but take into account respect for Mother Earth's expression of love for all her children, creeping, crawling, walking, flying and plant people. Flower essences have no direct impact on the body's biochemistry, as do pharmacological and psychoactive drugs. They do not, as modern medicines do, affect brain chemistry. There is no chemically induced mood altering with flower essences. They work on vibrational resonance rather than as a biochemical agent. Flower agents are catalysts to encourage inner dialogue with the visible/invisible self, or aid in changing consciousness. Hence, they are not prescribed as remedies to treat particular ailments but to compel the individual toward inner development to learn the lesson posed by the dis-ease.

Remedies are prepared to include all properties of the plant, not just the active agent, and they are selected not on the basis of physical and emotional qualities of the patient but on the basis of their impact on soul qualities, practitioners say.

The plants are gathered at the highest moment of their unfolding and only the blossoms are used; additionally, the environmental conditions of the plant are of utmost importance. For example, some of the finest essences being produced are coming from Alaska in an area free of pollution of any form and totally in their natural environment; though someone choosing to follow flower essence technology could draw from the shamanic experience in selecting plants from a home environment. (Simply journey out and ask the plants themselves!)

Other energy modalities that you are likely to encounter, and might want to look up on the Internet for more information are: acupuncture, shiatsu, tai chi, reflexology, polarity therapy, kinesiology, craniosacral, myofacial release, zero balancing, sound therapy, color therapy and energetic breathwork, or rebirthing.

Launching Yourself

This book, of course, is by no means a complete or encyclopedic compendium of energy medicine, Reiki or shamanism, but it is hoped that by having read this book, you will be prepared to launch yourself into the world — and worlds! — as a Reiki shaman. As I tell the students who come to me and learn to be Reiki masters, becoming a "master" isn't an end, but a beginning. It's a challenge to master yourself, which is a lifelong obligation. As a Reiki shaman, you will find your personal power grows immensely, and with it the obligation to comport yourself and act always with discernment.

Study, practice, and most of all, enjoy! Our sojourn in this Earth walk is all too brief to be encumbered with heavy thoughts and willful, rigid aspirations. Let your path be guided by the verities that the trees once told me:

> Allow, Accept, Acknowledge and Be Grateful!
> Many Blessings on Your Path *(Wisatologi Nihi)!*
> We are all related *(Gus di i da da dv ni)!*

Exercise 4 Finding Stone People To Help You

All "stone people," or Earth stones, have healing properties based on their individual makeup or vibrational qualities, and crystals don't have the corner on Power, with a capital "P," for dynamic spiritual effects. For example, today, when I do ceremonies, I usually will walk around the yard or parking lot of the place where I'm to do the work and see which stone people "call" to me. Those that make their intent known, that they want to help heal people, are the ones that are used in ceremony. Afterwards, I'll either give them back to the Earth or give them to whoever at the ceremony wants them. Often, those in attendance will say, "Where did you get these beautiful stones?" And I'll answer truthfully: "I found them out in the parking lot."

The same process goes for finding "grandfathers" for the Inipi (Lakota: sweat lodge) or Asi (Cherokee: hot house), where water is poured on heated stones for healing of the people. I go into a field or along a creek and ask: "Who wants to help the people heal?" And those stones that become luminous, almost magnetic in their attraction, seeming to suddenly distinguish themselves from their surroundings, are the ones chosen. In each case, when choosing a stone for personal healing, or a group, state your intent out loud, look for stones that then seem to "jump out" at you, and then give some tobacco or corn meal in its place in gratitude to the Earth for this gift, and to keep balance on the Earth for what was taken.

From The Energy Notebook: The Light Being's Daughter

Shortly before Thanksgiving 2006, something happened that was a source of great wonderment. A being appeared at my doorstep and, together, we birthed a new being into the world.

I was sitting on the front porch enjoying the evening shortly before going to bed. The night was dark, and crisp. Each morning, we had awakened with white frost sparkling on the ground, and this night, clear and cold, the stars in Orion sharply wheeling overhead, promised another such day.

The night was quiet, not a bird stirring, all put to bed and asleep, about 10 pm, and I noticed something looming out of the darkness. It was a being of some kind, a being of light. I stared in wonderment. What was this?

It came steadily closer until it stood at the foot of the front steps. Its intensity was so bright that I could make out no features. It felt feminine, was tall, about 7 feet perhaps, and slender, with no visible form except intense white light, no facial characteristics that could be determined, and where I perceived it might have hands was cradled to it a dark object, as black as night.

Taken by surprise, I felt fear tinge my awareness. Hello, I said, angel of light.

From within, communicating intuitively, it answered that it was not an angel. I have seen angels in journey and knew it was not; but I knew not what to call it. The blankness of my mind left the impression that what it was had no words in my knowledge or understanding, so it remained a Being of Light.

Thus confronted with this unknown thing, the tinge of fear still shivering me, I called to my power animals, which were close by, and saw them: the eagle above me, its wings sheltering; the owl off to the right, simply knowing, like a doorway into the unknown; the wolf standing off a bit to the front, silently watching; the bear behind me, more a comforting presence, than seen. With my power animals, knowing they were there, the fear melted away. I looked at the Being of Light, with a question: what do you want?

It held the bundle of darkness out to me and said, again not in words, but as a knowing in my mind: can you heal?

Again, the fear came. In my experience, and I've seen many things, when darkness is present, it's best left alone. When we venture into the unknown, we carry out own light, our own good medicine, *nvwati*, and it is that light of Creator that connects us with every thing, everything of Creator, the good medicine in all things. Where there is the absence of light, the absence of *nvwati*, it is best to leave it alone.

I looked at my power animals. They were totally neutral; all watching, but giving no sign of yea or nay; it was my decision.

I looked at this bundle of darkness that was being held out to me; it also had no features; just a bundle of darkness, as dark as was light with the Being of Light. Getting no clue from my power animals, I looked within myself and felt for an answer, reaching with a tendril of thought for the inner knowing that is our inherent wisdom. There was light there, and power, no fear, but neither a yea or nay. It was my decision.

I thought to myself: there is no reason not to heal. Healing is good. When connected with the highest light, the highest power, what can transpire can only be good. And so, without even thinking how, I reached out my hand toward this bundle of darkness and felt myself inwardly reach toward and connect with the Plume of Quetzcoatl (what some call The Christ Consciousness Grid), the place of highest light, highest power, that holds within it the highest good for all things, and felt the light pass through me, through my hands to this bundle of darkness.

The bundle began to transform. Out of its blackness, bands of light appeared. It appeared, at first, to me, as cat, like a striped tabby, the bands of light and darkness swirling to conform to shapes. But, then, a thought occurred in the back of my mind, that some Cherokee and some Choctaw call an owl "a cat with wings," and the bundle shifted again, with bands of gold appearing with the dark and light bands, until appearing from the swirl was the most beautiful owl I had ever seen. It had large, golden luminous eyes, with pupils black as night; it had bands of black and gold framing its face with the brightest silver edging, and the same gold and black bands with silver tinge across its entire body. It was alive; it was whole; it was complete: a beautiful, golden owl.

There, it is done, I said, putting down my hands.

The Being of Light looked down at this life form it cradled and said, with a voice of pure love, It belongs here with you.

Again, I was taken aback. What to do with this? Immediately, I knew I could not take it into the house. Its power was too great; it would shiver the place to pieces with its energy. So, I told the new being: You can stay here and protect the house.

The Being of Light left its bundle there, this golden creature, hovering in front of the porch, where it drifted off to one side, suspended in midair, and faded into the darkness as swiftly and as mysteriously as it had come.

I went inside the house and told my beautiful wife Waya what had happened. She was happy and excited, and we made images of the owl as nearly as we could approximate it, and hung them around the house so that it would feel supported and welcome.

When we retired for the night, I turned off the lights and it was brighter than day. Even with our eyes closed, the room was lit as if by an intense white light that threw no shadows. In the "darkness," I said to Waya lying by my side: Do you see how bright it is in here? She answered yes.

As I drifted off to sleep, the last thing I remember was seeing above us a sunset, with the sky in alternate bands of gold and dark clouds, as joyous a setting sun filling the sky as ever graced the Earth.

Since that night, I've pondered this event and come to some tentative conclusions. It occurred to me that this being was born of the Being of Light, but for whatever reason, it could not live in that intensity of light; in effect, still born. The mother, despairing of her offspring, looked around and saw me sitting on porch and "saw" that I knew how to heal or at least transfer energy in a good way, for life, for wholeness. And so, she revealed herself, in hope I could save her child, if not for life in her world, then for life itself.

It occurred to me that when I held out my hands to heal this thing, that I didn't connect with Reiki energy, which I usually do for healing, but instinctively connected with the highest good I could conceive: the Plume of Quetzalcoatl, which holds within it the possibilities of all things for the highest good, allowing this being to take what it needed, connected only with the highest and best energy.

And it occurred to me that the shape of the being was by my hand, as well; perhaps, unwittingly. As close as I could conceive, this being was like a Power of the Universe, like the power animals that hold close to me; among them, the owl — a being that literally "walks between the worlds." And this being, also, was given life so that it could "walk between the worlds," like the owl power animal. It is connected to this Earth because it could not live in the intensity of light of its mother, but it can live on a higher vibration than beings of this Earth; and so, it is the product and citizen of both: connected with the Earthly Mother and the Plume of Quetzalcoatl.

Since that night, I've glimpsed this being often. Usually, it's just a feeling, a presence, or perceiving that the "light' around the house is lighter than the rest of the area. One night, I came out on the porch and the being presented itself to me in a different way: it appeared up close as the form of a goddess in a flowing robe, all white, slender at the waist and its arms uplifted with great folds of light like puffy sleeves falling down — in short, appearing like its mother in all her glory. But if you pulled back, and squinted, as if from a distance, it appeared like the face of an owl — two large eyes where the puffy sleeves were, a narrow beak for its slender body. I could sense that it had been visiting its mother and so was closer to her vibration and appearance than that of the owl. And that made me glad; my heart soaring. It can be with its mother, communicate with her, be loved by her, and feel her love; and it can be here, too, in this world, healthy and whole, and not sickly or incomplete.

So, it lingers still, and I still puzzle over it. I have no idea what is this Being of Light, or its daughter. But I do know I was midwife to a miracle. And that makes my heart sing.

Aho.

Notes

Preface

1. Ascension Tests are the author's popular meditations/ observations that have been reprinted in newspapers, magazines and Web sites all over the world. They are designed to allow a broadening of understanding and perspective that at the same time raises one's vibration rate. An Ascension Test is included in each of the author's monthly newsletters, Keeping In Touch, that has subscribers across the United States and 23 foreign countries and on his Web site, Healing The Earth/ Ourselves, www.blueskywaters.com.

2. The author's three previous books are: *Clearing: A Guide for Liberating Energies Trapped in Buildings and Lands,* illustrated by Annette Waya Ewing, with a foreword by Brooke Medicine Eagle (Findhorn, Scotland: Findhorn Press, 2006); *Finding Sanctuary in Nature: Simple Ceremonies in the Native American Tradition for Healing Yourself and Others,* illustrated by Annette Waya Ewing (Findhorn, Scotland: Findhorn Press, 2007); and *Healing Plants and Animals from a Distance: Curative Principles and Applications* illustrated by Annette Waya Ewing (Findhorn, Scotland: Findhorn Press, 2007).

3. There are numerous lists online of Reiki masters available to give attunements; but I heartily recommend those who have been trained, attuned and follow the teachings and manuals by the International Center for Reiki Training, founded by William Lee Rand. For more information, contact the International Center for Reiki Training, 21421 Hilltop Street, Unit #28, Southfield, MI 48034. Phone:

800-332-8112. The ICRT's Web site is most informative, including lists of teachers and classes held around the United States and in other countries, and it offers beginner's materials for sale. See: http://www.reiki.org

Chapter One

1. There are many energetic systems that seek to describe the non-physical form of the body; the easiest is to simply see the physical form as the densest accretion or core of a layering of energetic shapes. Generally, it may be described as a body that exists beyond the physical plane; in humans such a body extends twenty-seven feet in each direction and thereafter continues into other dimensions.

2. *The Chakras, a Monograph* by C.W. Leadbeater (Wheaton, IL: The Theosophical Publishing House, 1968).

3. *The Serpent Power* by Arthur Avalon (Mineola, NY: Dover Publications, 1974)

4. *The Secret Doctrine* by H.P. Blavatsky (New York: Quest Books, 1988). For more information about how to guard against negative energies and to allow Earth energies (lower chakras) to aid in healing, growth and development, see "Grounding, Centering and Shielding" on our Web page: Healing The Earth/Ourselves, http://www.blueskywaters.com.

5. Carlos Castaneda, of course, has written many books about shamanism in which the energy body is seen as "a luminous egg," such as *The Teachings of Don Juan: A Yaqui Way of Knowledge* (New York: Ballantine, 1969). But his student, Ken Eagle Feather, has written a book focusing on the energy body that I recommend. See: *Toltec Dreaming: Don Juan's Teachings on the Energy Body* (Rochester, VT: Bear & Co., 2007).

6. See Drunvalo Melchizedek's books *Ancient Secrets of the Flower of Life,* vols. 1 and 2 (Flagstaff, AZ: Light Technology Publishing, 1990), which are taught in courses given by Flower of Life Research LLC, P.O. Box 55844, Phoenix, AZ 85078; phone: 602-996-0900; Web site: http://www.floweroflife.org. The books and courses are highly recommended.

7. See Melchizedek, *Ancient Secrets of the Flower of Life,* Vol. 2.

8. See *Wheels of Light: Chakras, Auras, and the Healing Energy of the Body* (Simon & Schuster; New York; 1989) by Rosalyn L. Brueyere.

9. For more on vibration and its effects, see the author's book *Healing Plants and Animals From a Distance: Curative Principles and Applications.*

10. In recent years, Gregg Braden, a geophysicist and author of *Awakening to Zero Point: The Collective Initiation* (Bellevue, WA: Radio Bookstore Press, 1997) and *Walking Between the Worlds: The Science of Compassion* (Bellevue, WA: Radio Bookstore Press, 1997), has hypothesized that the Earth is going through great changes with profound implications for its inhabitants, coinciding with ancient prophecies of the Egyptians, Hopi, Aztecs, and Mayans, as well as those found in the Christian Bible.

11. See the author's book, *Finding Sanctuary in Nature: Simple Ceremonies in the Native American Tradition for Healing Yourself and Others.*

12. See *Power vs. Force: The Hidden Determinants of Human Behavior* by David R. Hawkins, M.D., Ph.D. (Carlsbad, Calif.: Hays House, 1995).

13. For more on this, see the author's book *Healing Plants and Animals From a Distance: Curative Principles and Applications.*

14. For more on learning how to perceive reality, including vision quest, sweat lodge, etc, see the author's book, *Finding Sanctuary in Nature: Simple Ceremonies in the Native American Tradition for Healing Yourself and Others.*

15. For more on the star tetrahedron and the energy body, see Melchizedek, Note 7; also see the author's book *Healing Plants and Animals From a Distance: Curative Principles and Applications.*

16. See Melchizedek, Note 7.

Chapter Two

1. Although Sensei (Japanese: teacher) Usui was not a trained physician in the modern sense, he was a healer and operated a clinic in Japan, so we respect him with the honorific of "Dr."

2. *The Dead Sea Scrolls: A New Translation* by Michael Wise, et al.; (New York: HarperSanFrancisco, 1996).

3. See Maureen J. Kelly, *Reiki and the Healing Buddha* (Twin Lakes, WI; Lotus Press, 2000); also, Note 2.

4. Various ancient Egyptian practices are associated with what is believed to be Reiki practice, regarding use of the Ankh. A mural on the wall at Abu Simbel shows Isis, Horus and Osiris with an oddly shaped staff that apparently is being used to "tune" the chakras, and is believed to be a depiction of giving a Reiki attunement. Today, many who receive attunements report having past-life memories of being attuned in ancient Egypt and other places; it's believed that many who receive attunements in this lifetime are drawn to do so because they already have the pathways open and the embodied memory of what it's like to heal with the hands. See Chapter 1, Note 7.

5. Reiki attunement is not limited to "Reiki" per se; it has many names in many cultures; it's likely various Native American healing techniques stem from similar "universal energy," the umane (ooo-mah-nay, Lakota: Earth energy), being the most obvious. Umane is power of the Earth in its raw state and is employed in various ceremonies, both as a symbol and as a practice or activity; see the author's books, *Finding Sanctuary in Nature: Simple Ceremonies in the Native American Tradition for Healing Yourself and Others* and *Healing Plants and Animals From a Distance: Curative Principles and Applications.*

6. *The Spirit of Reiki* by Walter Lubeck, Frank Arjava Petter, William Lee Rand (Twin Lakes, WI; Lotus Press, 2002).

7. *Reiki: The Legacy of Dr. Usui* by Frank Arjava Petter, (Twin Lakes, WI: Shangri-La Press, 1998)

8. See Petter, *Reiki: The Legacy of Dr. Usui.*

9. *The Original Reiki Handbook of Dr. Mikao Usui* by Dr. Mikao Usui and Frank Arjava Petter (Twin Lakes, WI; Lotus Press, 1999).

10. See Usui, Petter, *The Original Reiki Handbook of Dr. Mikao Usui.*

11. For more on the fast, or pipe fast, see the author's book, *Finding Sanctuary in Nature: Simple Ceremonies in the Native American Tradition for Healing Yourself and Others.*

12. *The Spirit of Reiki* by Lubeck, et al.; also see the books, writings, lectures and tapes of Rand, and the ICRT, Preface, Note 3.

13. For more on ceremonies using these Powers, see the author's book *Finding Sanctuary in Nature: Simple Ceremonies in the Native American Tradition for Healing Yourself and Others.*

14. See Lubeck's "The Meaning of the Reiki Character" in *The Spirit of Reiki,* Note 6.

15. For a more detailed line-by-line discussion, see Lubeck, Note 14.

16. Reiki does not conflict at all with the practice of Christianity. In fact, there's a Web site titled "Reiki for Christians" created by Christians for Christians who practice Reiki dedicated to explaining how Reiki fits perfectly with its practice, and as a place to share ideas and experiences. See: http://www.christianreiki.org/

17. For more on non-Reiki healing techniques, including using the hands and long-distance, see the author's book *Healing Plants and Animals From a Distance: Curative Principles and Applications.*

18. I've often had students ask me if I will do some Reiki for someone because they are ill, depressed or not feeling well and I point out: what better way is there to help someone than by helping yourself? By practicing Reiki, one raises one's vibration rate, accelerating the healing process. If performing hands-on Reiki on someone while ill, or depressed, make sure — as one should always do anyway in treating someone energetically — to ground, center and shield during the treatment, and use an affirmation afterwards of thanking Creator for removing all footprints and debris from yourself and the other person and returning them where they belong.

19. See www.reiki.org, or the the ICRT, Preface, Note 3,

20. See Preface, Note 3.

21. For more on Karuna Reiki® and its symbols, see www.reiki.org, or the the ICRT, Preface, Note 3, or our Web site, www.blueskywaters.com. For more on other symbols frequently used in Reiki, see the book by Diane Stein, *Essential Reiki: A Complete Guide to an Ancient Healing Art* (Freedom, Calif.: The Crossing Press; 1995).

22. For more on this, see our Web site: Healing The Earth/Ourselves, www.blueskywaters.com, under "Grounding, Centering and Shielding."

23. See Stein, *Essential Reiki: A Complete Guide to an Ancient Healing Art.*

24. This technique, called the Gassho Meditation, is taught by William Lee Rand, see Preface, Note 3.

25. See Peter V. Catches's Web site: http://www. ocetiwakan.org. He has written a book, *Sacred Fireplace: Life and Teachings of a Lakota Medicine Man* (Santa Fe, NM: Clear Light Publishing, 1999), and a Lakota language book and CD is sold on his Web site to fund his charitable work. Catches (Zintkala Oyate), a descendent of thirty-seven generations of medicine men, is Keeper of the Spotted Eagle Way of Lakota medicine, its oral history, sacred rites, and experiential teachings. He has conducted the Spotted Eagle Sun Dance at his home on the Pine Ridge Reservation in South Dakota for twenty-eight consecutive years.

Chapter Three

1. The first representational art of Europe is dated at 30,000 years ago, with anthropomorphic images, such as the lion/man figure from Hohlenstein-Stadel in Germany. Totemism and anthropomorphic thinking, both universal to shamanism, can thus be conclusively derived from that date, although shamanic practices probably extend far earlier. For more, see "Explaining The Early Human Mind" by Steve Mithen, *British Archaeology,* No. 15, June 1996.

2. *The Dancing Wu Li Masters: An Overview of the New Physics* by Gary Zukov. (New York: William Morrow, 1979).

3. *The Tao of Physics* by Fritjof Capra (Berkeley, Calif.: Shambala, 1975).

4. *Wholeness and the Implicate Order* by David Bohm (Boston: Routledge & Kegan Paul, 1980).

5. See the book by Rupert Sheldrake, *A New Science of Life* (Los Angeles: J P Tarcher, 1982).

6. To learn more about soul retrieval, see Sandra Ingerman's book, *Soul Retrieval: Mending the Fragmented Self* (San Francisco: Harper, 1991). Sandra taught me soul retrieval and it's one of the mainstays of my practice. She teaches classes on soul retrieval through The Foundation for Shamanic Studies. For more information, contact the Foundation for Shamanic Studies, P.O. Box 1939, Mill Valley, CA 94942. Phone: 415-380-8282. Web site: http://www.shamanism.org Amongst the courses offered by the Foundation for Shamanic Studies, I recommend those taught by Dana Robinson. He has facilitated well over 500 workshops for the Foundation over the last 20+ years. A graduate of the University of Maryland, he has explored several spiritual paths and has studied extensively with Michael Harner, founder of the FSS, and also with Brazilian Spiritists, the Tuvan shamans, and an Ulchi shaman. He is also a Harner Method Shamanic Counselor and Founder of The Next Step Shamanic Program. Also, see Alberto Villoldo's Four Winds Society at http://www.thefourwinds.org. and Ingerman's book, *Shamanic Journeying: A Beginner's Guide* (Boulder, CO: Sounds True, 2004), which includes a drumming CD and simple instructions. She also offers classes based on her book *Medicine for the Earth: How to Transform Personal and Environmental Toxins*. You may write to obtain a schedule of her Medicine for the Earth workshops at P.O. Box 4757, Santa Fe, NM 87502. Or visit her Web site: http://www. shamanicvisions.com We also offer more information on our Web site, Healing the Earth/Ourselves, www. blueskywaters.com. Additionally, a variety of shamanic drumming books, CDs, training, etc., are offered by Michael Drake, Talking Drum Publications: http://www.

geocities.com/talkingdrumpub He offers a free newsletter, The Talking Drum, which is most useful.

7. For more on complementary and alternative medicine, including a Power Point presentation, see our Web site, www.blueskywaters.com. See also: James L. Oschman and Nora H. Oschman, *Readings on the Scientific Basis of Bodywork, Energetic and Movement Therapies* (Dover, N.H.: N.O.R.A. Press, 1999).

8. For more on Native American spiritual practices, see the author's books, *Finding Sanctuary in Nature: Simple Ceremonies in the Native American Tradition for Healing Yourself and Others* and *Healing Plants and Animals From a Distance: Curative Principles and Applications.*

9. For more on this, see *The Tibetan Book of Living and Dying* by Sogyal Rinpoche (New York: Harper, 1994) and *The Tibetan Book of the Dead* by Padma Sambhava and Robert A. Thurman (New York: Bantam, 1994). The body of knowledge commonly referred to as the "book" of the dead or a variant is actually a written form of the recited mantra traditionally given bedside for the deceased to help negotiate the afterlife. It is meant to take three days, or 72 hours, to recite: the amount of time a spirit lingers in this plane –useful to know for those who are guided to do psychopomp, or helping souls to the afterlife. Although it's culture specific, that is, filled with deities that might only be seen by someone who grew up in Tibetan culture, it is useful for Western readers in that it offers a glimpse of the sights, sounds, visions and activities that may occur immediately after death.

10. See The Infancy Gospels of James and Thomas: *The Scholars Bible* by Ronald F. Hock, (Santa Barbara, Calif.: Polebridge Press, 1995), also Hock's *The Life of Mary and the Birth of Jesus: The Ancient Infancy Gospel of James* (Berkeley, Calif.: Ulysses Press, 1997).

11. *The Nag Hammadi Library* by James M. Robinson, et al.; Revised Edition (New York: HarperSanFrancisco, 1990).

12. These techniques are taught by the Foundation for Shamanic Studies, see Note 6, also by the International Center For Reiki Training, see Preface, Note 3.

13. For more on the qualities of time, especially in its mutability during spiritual ceremonies, see the author's books, *Finding Sanctuary in Nature: Simple Ceremonies in the Native American Tradition for Healing Yourself and Others* and *Healing Plants and Animals From a Distance: Curative Principles and Applications*.

14. The Native American teachings of The Pale One are carried on to this day by Dhyani Ywahoo, a Cherokee (Tsalagi) teacher, who explains many of the concepts in her book, *Voices of the Ancestors: Cherokee Teachings from the Wisdom Fire* (Boston: Shambhala Publications, 1987). In 1969, her Sunray Meditation Society was founded as a vehicle for the appropriate teachings of the Ywahoo lineage to be shared with those of one heart, and today students and practitioners of the Sunray teachings are flourishing as seeds of light and right relationship in communities throughout Turtle Island (North America) and the world. See her Web site: http://www.sunray.org.

15. *The Secret Teachings of Jesus: Four Gnostic Gospels* by Marvin W. Meyer (New York: Vintage Books, 1986).

16. *Black Elk Speaks: Being the Life Story of a Holy Man of the Oglala Sioux* by John G. Neihardt (Lincoln: University of Nebraska Press, 2000).

17. See Note 6.

18. For more on learning the songs of plants, see the author's book *Healing Plants and Animals From a Distance: Curative Principles and Applications*.

19. Drumming CDs and tapes are available commercially from a variety of sources, see Note 6.

20. *Journey To Ixtlan: The Lessons of Don Juan* by Carlos Castaneda (New York: Simon & Schuster, 1977).

21. One of my activities is the Bear Dance, a spiritual practice like Sundance, whereby the dancers take on the illnesses of the people in attendance and all beings to some extent, by dancing the Bear. Through ceremony, we become the Bear, the spirit of Bear, and so it's the Power of the Bear that heals. The dancers themselves practice clearing and cleansing techniques upon themselves, primarily Inipi/Asi (sweat lodge) for purification before and after the dance and during the dance the dancers are constantly bathed in sage smoke to keep them in spirit and prevent the diseases from attaching to them while the Bear Spirit transmutes the dis-eases. This should only be done after intense spiritual training and experience. For more on the Bear Dance, see our Web site www.blueskywaters.com

22. For more on healing plants (and animals), see the author's book *Healing Plants and Animals From a Distance: Curative Principles and Applications.*

23. Michael Drake, the author of *The Shamanic Drum: A Guide to Sacred Drumming and I Ching: The Tao of Drumming,* has a free newsletter, The Talking Drum, and a Web page featuring articles, books and workshops, see: http://www. geocities.com/talkingdrumpub

Chapter Four

1. I have been told that, as a practitioner of Native American spiritual healing, I should not have people fill out a client form, just do the work. If people lived in the 19th century and all the people who came to me were members of my tribe, who I had known from birth, the form might not be necessary, and taking "payment" in the form of blankets,

tobacco, etc, would be perfectly adequate. But this is the 21st century. People come to me from all walks of life and with every imaginable expectation. I practice in the modern world, and I keep records and accept payment like everyone else (though we do not charge for ceremony, in keeping with tradition). For awhile, early in my career, I accepted any "gift of the heart" as payment, but found myself constantly without funds, even having to pay for gasoline to go do work for people.

When I married, my wife wondered how in the world I had accumulated so many blankets. I told her someone had once said that medicine men are paid in blankets; so this was why. Just about everything in my house was something someone had given for treatment, including, my favorite, a broken artificial Christmas tree. For the first year of our marriage, I think my wife spent a lot of her time throwing out these "gifts of the heart," a lot of which, frankly, were items nobody wanted. In actuality, the tradition of "pay" or gift giving for medicine men, healers, has been corrupted in modern life. Among the Tsalagi (Cherokee), such remuneration was called *ugista 'ti* — an archaic word meaning, literally, "for to eat." Without these gifts, a medicine man, or woman, couldn't have time to practice medicine, or survive. As Peter V. Catches, a 38th generation Lakota medicine man has said, "in the old days there was not money so a person gave something of great value to help them. Just to talk to a medicine man they would bring him a horse. Later on as blankets were of great value to them, they would give a medicine man some blankets. Today's form of barter is usually money. What is wrong with that?" For more on this, see our Web site, Healing The Earth Ourselves, www.blueskywaters.com under Ugista 'ti: The Pay of Medicine Men. There should be an exchange of energy for balance in the relationship. For more on Catches, see Note 25, Chapter 2.

2.   For more on drumming CDs, see Note 6, Chapter 3.

3.   The essence of protecting yourself from psychic attacks is to not be duped into believing that you are vulnerable; you are not. If encountered, brujos, sorcerers, or any malignant entities might attempt to trick you into believing you are already vulnerable or under their control or harmed by them. If you believe it, then you have given them your power and opened the door for further attacks. With your power animals and Creator's Power, you are invulnerable. Certain techniques can be employed to bounce back from psychic attack and protect home and property. This issue is dealt with in more depth in the author's books *Finding Sanctuary in Nature: Simple Ceremonies in the Native American Tradition for Healing Yourself and Others,* and *Clearing: A Guide for Liberating Energies Trapped in Buildings and Lands.*

4.   To smudge, light the smudge stick of sage, sweetgrass, cedar or other medicinal herbs, available from most health food stores, and then start rattling with one hand while moving the smudge stick so the smoke covers the area before you. This clears the space energetically, and raises the vibration rate. For more on this, see the author's previous books, *Clearing: A Guide to Liberating Energies Trapped in Buildings and Lands* and *Finding Sanctuary in Nature: Simple Ceremonies in the Native American Tradition for Healing Yourself and Others*. Some people have difficulty breathing smoke of any kind, and in some places fire restrictions may apply. We often use liquid smudge, which is herbal essences in liquid form. We recommend Blue Eagle Invocation™ Liquid Smudge. For more about it, see our Web page, www.blueskywaters.com

5.   Experiencing your own death is a frequent shamanic initiation, sometimes experienced through being dismembered by a power animal and put back together, so that a more spiritual life can be experienced, sometimes intentionally done through the shamanic journey.

Generally, though, a power animal will not allow one to pass into physical death; only through a dispensation by higher powers is this accomplished, and it's not advisable to try. The beauty of the "other side" is such that one might not want to return and when it's intentionally done, people expertly trained in shamanism should be available and ready to retrieve the person and bring him or her back, if required.

6. For more on the use of crystals in ceremonies, see the author's book *Finding Sanctuary in Nature: Simple Ceremonies in the Native American Tradition for Healing Yourself and Others.*

7. A useful compendium of healing properties of stones is *Love is in the Earth* By Melody (Wheat Ridge, CO: Earth-Love Publishing House, 1995).

8. Mt. Ida, Ark., billed as "The Crystal Capital of the World," is a great place to find crystals and learn about digging for them. The people there depend on tourism, so they are very helpful. For more, see our Web site, www.blueskywaters.com

9. *USA Today,* Nov. 4, 2007, "Healing touch: A new patient outreach program." For more on complementary, alternative medicine, or CAM modalities, see our Web site's PowerPoint presentation on CAM Facts, www.blueskywaters.com. Also, see the ICRT's Web site on Reiki in hospitals: www.reiki.org

10. For specific techniques for accessing the body's inherent wisdom, see the author's book *Finding Sanctuary in Nature: Simple Ceremonies in the Native American Tradition for Healing Yourself and Others.*

11. *Your Inner Physician and You* by Dr. John E. Upledger (Berkeley, Calif.: North Atlantic Books,1997). Dr. Upledger has a non-profit organization, The Upledger Foundation, 11211 Prosperity Farms Rd., Palm Beach Gardens, FL

33410-3487, which offers information, treatment and training.

12. For more on navigating the plant nations, see the author's book *Healing Plants and Animals From a Distance: Curative Principles and Applications.*

13. To learn more about stone properties and view Annette Waya Ewing's necklaces, see Bear Walks With Wolf Studios on the Web site, www.blueskywaters.com

14. See Note 6, Chapter 1.

15. Stanislav Grof's organization is: Grof Transpersonal Training, Inc., PMB 516, 38 Miller Ave., Mill Valley, CA 94941. For more information, see the Web site: www.holotropic.com

Glossary

allies. Wild spirits of the land that can aid in healing and protecting natural habitats.

all-time, no-time. The present, accessed at its deepest level.

angels. Emissaries of light of divine origin who accompany humans through life and are available for assistance and inspiration.

animus. The spark of life.

antahkarana. Ancient healing symbol, thousands of years old, that can be used for local and long-distance healing.

archetypes. Attributes existing in potential form that can be brought into manifestation; original models after which other similar things are patterned.

ascension. Transcending to a higher level of consciousness; the next step in human and planetary evolution.

assemblage points. The areas in energy body that "connect" us to what we perceive as reality, both with our senses, and beyond our senses, to ground us into a reality we can perceive and understand.

aura. Emanations of the energy body, often seen as colors that show moods, thoughts, or potentials; energetic fields surrounding the physical body, including physical, etheric, emotional, mental, astral, etheric template, celestial, and causal.

authentic self. Who you really are, not who you think you are, or have been told you are by outside sources.

brujo. Witch, masculine form, Spanish (feminine *bruja;* masculine plural *brujos;* feminine plural *brujas).*

centering. Locating the core of consciousness in the body; drawing magnetic energy from the earth and electrical energy from the sun to operate with balanced awareness.

chakra. Sanskrit for circle or wheel; the energetic centers in the core of the body linked together by a central psychic energy channel.

Christ Consciousness Grid (also called the Plume of Quetzalcoatl). An energy layer surrounding the earth that signifies the earth's highest potential and that was supposedly established by higher beings, often referred to as ascended beings, to help humanity through the current "shift of the ages."

cleansing. Transmuting energy to a higher, more positive form by raising its vibrational rate.

clearing. Dissipating (transmuting) negative energy. Clearing spaces usually also cleanses them since the act of clearing raises the vibrational rate.

co-creating. Operating as a partner with the Creator to boost positive energy.

ego. The survival mechanism, which is part of the personality. See personality.

energy. Subtle power manifested through life force, frequency, or cohesion.

energy body. A body that exists beyond the physical plane; in humans, such a body extends twenty-seven feet in each direction and thereafter continues into other dimensions. See aura.

fast. See vision quest.

fractal. A geometric pattern repeated at ever smaller scales to produce shapes and surfaces that cannot be represented by classical geometry but can recreate irregular patterns and structures in nature.

flow of creation. The movement or stasis of energy in a given moment.

God vs. Creator. God is one, all; the Creator is the active aspect of God as expressed in the will of creation.

goddesses. Land spirits of the highest order, usually associated with a place or characteristic; also, humans who have transcended but chosen to remain on earth in spirit form as a means of service.

grounding. Connecting with the earth energetically to ensure that consciousness is not operating from other dimensions or overly affected by other energetic forces.

guides. Spirit helpers, soul brothers or sisters from former or future lifetimes, or spiritual masters who have assumed a supportive role for a particular soul's evolution.

heart song, or power song. A song that expresses the unique, positive energies, traits, and intents of an individual, usually discovered through fasting and prayer.

higher power. God as expressed through one's highest nature.

kachinas. Supernatural beings revered by the Hopi and appearing as messengers from the spirit world; spirit beings; objects that may be crafted to represent the spirit body of beings.

lela wakan. Lakota term meaning "very sacred."

ley lines. Grids that crisscross the earth and hold potential electromagnetic energy, many of which were identified by ancient peoples, who built sacred sites over them.

life-force energy. Energy that is all around us in nature and that is emitted by the earth.

light body. Energetic body; the quality of energy around a person, as opposed to their physical body. See MerKaBa.

matter. Patterns of energy we perceive as having substance.

medicine. The inherent power within all things.

medicine wheel. A Native American system of prayer, meditation, and discovery, recognizing that life follows a circle. The wheel's directions and their significance, concepts from which all things are said to derive, include east (newness, discovery), south (youth, growth, healing), west (introspection, setting sun, light within), north (wisdom, elders, ancestors), center (soul, spirit), above (Heavenly Father), and below (Earth Mother).

meridians. Lines along the body where energy is channeled; often used in acupuncture and other energy medicine to effect healing.

MerKaBa. In sacred geometry, a star tetrahedron; an energetic framework that forms a blueprint for spirit to attach and from which, in plants and animals, DNA creates a physical expression; a geometric form that includes the light body; a pattern of energy shared by animals, plants, stones, and all objects, including those that are man-made.

mind of God. Expansion of human thought to higher consciousness as far as is conceivable.

morphogenic field. A universal field encoding the basic pattern of an object. From the Greek *morphe,* which means form, and *genesis,* which denotes coming into being. Noncorporeal beings manifest in three-dimensional reality through morphogenic resonance.

nagual. In Toltec shamanism, what is really real (nonordinary reality), as opposed to what we think is real according to our consensus reality; everything that can be. See tonal.

native peoples. Indigenous cultures practicing traditional nature-based ways.

nonordinary reality. Reality as seen when everyday constraints and predispositions are eliminated through trance or other methods.

personality. All that we adhere to, or believe, that makes us who we think we are. See ego.

pipe fast. See vision quest.

portal. A vortex through which objects and entities can pass from one dimension of reality to another while realm shifting.

power animal. An animal that offers guidance and protection; a totem.

power song, or heart song. A song that expresses the unique, positive energies, traits, and intents of an individual, usually discovered through fasting and prayer.

power spot. A place where all energies of a structure or tract of land are focused.

prana. Universal life-force energy.

prayer stick. A stick, either ornate or plain, that has been consecrated through prayer; wrapped with cloth, ribbon, or yarn; and most often, planted in the ground to carry a prayer.

rattling. Shaking a rattle to break up energy or bring in energy.

realm shifting. The movement of objects between dimensions; while some objects, such as quartz crystals, do this routinely because of their energetic composition, others will disappear and reappear only when near a portal.

Reiki. A Japanese form of energy medicine involving sacred symbols and guides; use of the hands to channel healing energy.

sacred circle. All beings in our lives — past, present, and future — who are connected to us; consecrated circle for ceremony.

self-talk. The inner dialogue inside our minds; the "what ifs," "buts," judgments, and fears that prevent us from being who we really are.

shaman. Siberian word meaning "one who sees in the dark"; a person who uses earth energy, guides, and power animals for insight; a medicine man or woman.

shielding. Creating, through intent, a protective energy layer around you to deflect external negative energy.

shift of the ages. Powerful changes in energy patterns now occurring on earth as a prelude to earth transformations and humanity's eventual development of higher consciousness.

skan. Lakota word, meaning power of the wind; a sacred force of movement; that which existed before God; life-force energy; the principle that manifests prayers from prayer flags.

smudging. Burning a plant such as sage, cedar, or sweetgrass to purify the energy of an area.

soul. The essential life force, or essence, of a being that is eternal from lifetime to lifetime.

soul retrieval. The act of retrieving soul parts, or essence, lost through trauma or stolen by another individual.

space. Any defined area, including the objects within it.

spiral of ascension. Spiral of life that offers a changing perspective as new lessons are encountered and old ones repeated, until the lessons are finally learned.

spirit. The essential quality of a being as an expression of soul; noncorporeal aspect of a person aligned with their soul purpose.

spirit quest. Following only what spirit dictates, usually over the course of days.

star beings. Beings from the stars whom cultures around the globe and throughout time have claimed influenced human development and who are honored at some sacred spots.

stillpoint. An inner place of total silence and stillness, where intuition and creativity originate and balance can be found; the source of being.

tesseract. A hypercube, also called the 8-cell or octachoron; sacred geometry shape for ceremony, frequently depicted in art as the shape of angels.

thought forms. Organized patterns of energy, either free floating or embedded in a space, that can be broken up by rattling or other means of transmutation.

tonal. In Toltec shamanism, the idea of what is real (our common, consensus reality), in contrast to what is really real (nonordinary reality), the nagual. See nagual.

transmutation. Changing energy from one state to another, such as transforming water to ice or vapor and vice versa; changing negative, or inert, energy into positive, or active, energy; or neutralizing energy to be reabsorbed by the earth. Ancient practices involved burying an energized object in the ground, burning it with fire, or submerging it in water.

umane. (Lakota: OO-Mah-ne) Sacred symbol of Earth energy in its raw form, often depicted in stone pictographs as a square with lines of energy from each corner, or as a square with enlongated corners to represent power coming from and going out to all corners of the universe.

unoli (You-Know-Lee). Cherokee, meaning literally "winds" but used as a designation for the powers of the directions.

vibrational rate/vibrational frequency. The measurable level of energy of a person, place, or object; the higher the rate, the closer to the source, or optimal wholeness.

vision quest. A period of time spent in a desolate or isolated spot under the tutelage of a spiritual elder, intended as an opportunity for discovering the inner self, the meaning of life, or to connect with higher beings.

vortexes. Doorways or portals into other dimensions; areas where energy in flux can affect time and space.

wakan. Lakota word meaning "sacred."

Wakan-Tanka. Lakota word for Great Spirit, or the Great Mystery, God.

wand. A long, thin implement used to direct energy when pointed. Some are ornate, with carvings, feathers, beads, and similar adornments, while others are as simple as a twig or a feather.

wild spirit. A spirit of the land that usually inhabits wilderness areas away from civilization or contact with humans; ally.

will of creation. Energy of the moment, moving from one state to another; the potential to transform to another manifestation.

Bibliography

Avalon, Arthur. *The Serpent Power*. Mineola, NY: Dover Publications, 1974.

Blavatsky, H.P. *The Secret Doctrine*. New York: Quest Books, 1988.

Bohm, David. *Wholeness and the Implicate Order*. Boston: Routledge & Kegan Paul, 1980.

Braden, Gregg. *Awakening to Zero Point: The Collective Initiation*. Bellevue, WA: Radio Bookstore Press, 1997.

——. *Walking Between the Worlds: The Science of Compassion*. Bellevue, WA: Radio Bookstore Press, 1997.

Brueyere, Rosalyn L. *Wheels of Light: Chakras, Auras, and the Healing Energy of the Body*. New York: Simon & Schuster, 1989.

Capra, Fritjof. *The Tao of Physics*. Berkeley, Calif.: Shambala, 1975.

Castaneda, Carlos. *Journey To Ixtlan: The Lessons of Don Juan*. New York: Simon & Schuster, 1977.

——. *The Teachings of Don Juan: A Yaqui Way of Knowledge*. New York: Ballantine,

Catches, Pete S., Sr., Peter V. Catches, ed. *Sacred Fireplace (Oceti Wakan): Life and Teachings of a Lakota Medicine Man*. Santa Fe, NM: Clear Light Publishers, 1999.

Desy, Phylameana lila. *The Everything Reiki Book: Channel Your Positive Energy to Reduce Stress, Promote Healing, and Enhance Your Quality of Life.* Cincinnati, OH: Adams Media Corporation, 2004.

Drake, Michael. *The Shamanic Drum: A Guide to Sacred Drumming.* Mt. Angel, OR: Talking Drum Publications, 1991.

———. *I Ching: The Tao of Drumming.* Mt. Angel, OR: Talking Drum Publications, 2003.

Eagle Feather, Ken. *A Toltec Path.* Charlottesville, VA: Hampton Roads, 1995.

———. *Toltec Dreaming: Don Juan's Teachings on the Energy Body* (Rochester, VT: Bear & Co., 2007).

Ewing, Jim PathFinder. *Clearing: A Guide to Liberating Energies Trapped in Buildings and Lands.* Findhorn, Scotland: Findhorn Press, 2006.

———. *Finding Sanctuary in Nature: Simple Ceremonies in the Native American Tradition of Healing Yourself and Others,* Scotland: Findhorn Press, 2007.

———. *Healing Plants and Animals From a Distance: Curative Principles and Applications,* Scotland: Findhorn Press, 2007.

Gaia, Laurelle Shanti. *The Book On Karuna Reiki®.* Harsel, CO: Infinite Light Healing Studies Center Inc., 2001.

Harner, Michael. *The Way of the Shaman.* New York: Harper, 1980.

Hawkins, David R., M.D., Ph.D. *Power vs. Force: The Hidden Determinants of Human Behavior.* Carlsbad, Calif.: Hays House, 1995.

Hock, Ronald F. *The Infancy Gospels of James and Thomas: The Scholars Bible*. Santa Barbara, Calif.: Polebridge Press, 1995.

——. *The Life of Mary and the Birth of Jesus: The Ancient Infancy Gospel of James*. Berkeley, Calif. Ulysses Press, 1997.

Ingerman, Sandra. *Medicine for the Earth: How to Transform Personal and Environmental Toxins*. New York: Three Rivers Press, 2000.

——. *Shamanic Journeying: A Beginner's Guide*. Boulder, CO: Sounds True, 2004.

——. *Soul Retrieval: Mending the Fragmented Self*. San Francisco: Harper, 1991.

——. *Welcome Home: Following Your Soul's Journey Home*. San Francisco: Harper, 1993.

Kelly, Maureen J. *Reiki and the Healing Buddha*. Twin Lakes, WI: Lotus Press, 2000.

Leadbeater, C.W. *The Chakras, a Monograph*. Wheaton, IL: The Theosophical Publishing House, 1968.

Lubeck, Walter, and Frank Arjava Petter, William Lee Rand. *The Spirit of Reiki*. Twin Lakes, WI: Lotus Press, 2002.

Lungold, Ian Xel. *Mayan Calendar and Conversion Codex*. Sedona, AZ: Majix, 1999.

Medicine Eagle, Brooke. *The Last Ghost Dance: A Guide for Earth Mages*. New York: Wellspring/Ballantine, 2000.

——. *Buffalo Woman Comes Singing*. New York: Ballantine Books, 1991.

Melchizedek, Drunvalo. *Ancient Secrets of the Flower of Life,* vols. 1 and 2. Flagstaff, AZ: Light Technology Publishing, 1990.

Melody. *Love Is In The Earth: A kaleidoscope of Crystals.* Wheat Ridge, Colo.: Earth-Love Publishing House, Ltd., 1995.

Meyer, Marvin W. *The Secret Teachings of Jesus: Four Gnostic Gospels.* New York: Vintage Books, 1986.

Neihardt, John G. *Black Elk Speaks: Being the Life Story of a Holy Man of the Oglala Sioux.* Lincoln: University of Nebraska Press, 2000.

Oschman, James L., and Nora H. *Readings on the Scientific Basis of Bodywork, Energetic and Movement Therapies.* Dover, N.H.: N.O.R.A. Press, 1999.

Pert, Candace B., Ph.D. *Molecules of Emotion: The Science Behind Mind-Body Medicine.* New York: Simon & Schuster, 1999.

Petter, Frank Arjava. *Reiki: The Legacy of Dr. Usui.* Twin Lakes, WI: Shangri-La Press, 1998.

——, and Usui, Dr. Mikao. *The Original Reiki Handbook of Dr. Mikao Usui.* Twin Lakes, WI: Lotus Press, 1999.

Rand, William Lee. *Reiki: The Healing Touch: First and Second Degree Manual.* Southfield, Mich.: Vision Publications, 1991.

Rinpoche, Sogyal. *The Tibetan Book of Living and Dying.* New York: Harper, 1994.

Sambhava, Padma, and Robert A. Thurman (trans). *The Tibetan Book of the Dead.* New York: Bantam, 1994.

Robinson, James M., et al. *The Nag Hammadi Library.* New York: HarperSanFrancisco, 1990.

Sheldrake, Rupert. *A New Science of Life.* Los Angeles: J P Tarcher, 1982.

Stein, Diane. *Essential Reiki: A Complete Guide to an Ancient Healing Art.* Freedom, Calif.: The Crossing Press, 1995.

Upledger, John E. *Your Inner Physician and You.* Berkeley, Calif.: North Atlantic Books, 1997.

Weil, Andrew, M.D. *Sound Body, Sound Mind: Music for Healing with Dr. Andrew Weil* (Audio CD). Burbank, CA: Rhino Records, 2005.

Wise, Michael, et al. *The Dead Sea Scrolls: A New Translation.* New York: HarperSanFrancisco, 1996.

Ywahoo, Dhyani. *Voices of the Ancestors: Cherokee Teachings from the Wisdom Fire.* Boston: Shambhala Publications, 1987.

Zukov, Gary. *The Dancing Wu Li Masters: An Overview of the New Physics.* New York: William Morrow, 1979.

About the Author

Jim PathFinder Ewing (Nvnehi Awatisgi) is a Reiki Master teacher who also teaches shamanism in Lena, Mississippi, where he lives with his wife, Annette Waya Ewing. He travels extensively, giving workshops, classes, and lectures, and is available for consultation. To receive a schedule of workshops he teaches or sponsors, please write to:

> Jim PathFinder Ewing
> P.O. Box 387
> Lena, MS 39094

To subscribe to his free monthly online newsletter, Keeping in Touch, visit his Website, Healing the Earth/Ourselves, at http://www.blueskywaters.com

green press INITIATIVE

Findhorn Press is committed to preserving ancient forests and natural resources. We elected to print this title on 30% post consumer recycled paper, processed chlorine free. As a result, for this printing, we have saved:

> 9 Trees (40' tall and 6-8" diameter)
> 3,411 Gallons of Wastewater
> 7 million BTU's of Total Energy
> 438 Pounds of Solid Waste
> 822 Pounds of Greenhouse Gases

Findhorn Press made this paper choice because our printer, Thomson-Shore, Inc., is a member of Green Press Initiative, a nonprofit program dedicated to supporting authors, publishers, and suppliers in their efforts to reduce their use of fiber obtained from endangered forests.

For more information, visit www.greenpressinitiative.org

Environmental impact estimates were made using the Environmental Defense Paper Calculator. For more information visit: www.papercalculator.org.